To my family and dear friends....thank you for your support, love and advice throughout the process of writing this book. Those of you who read the early version of the book and gave me advice....thank you! I am humbled that you would do that for me. Thank you to my two children for your support and for the constant joy you continue to provide in my life. And, finally, to my sweet husband, Brent, who tells me every day that I can do whatever I set my sights on....your support and gentle nudging to keep me moving forward are never forgotten and always appreciated.

Thank you all...

<u>Introduction</u>

The razor-sharp blade was only inches from my face. My attacker stood before me, waving the cold steel back and forth menacingly, screaming at the top of his lungs, his neck veins bulging, his eyes full of fury and hatred, poised to strike. My heart was pounding in my chest, and terrified, I prayed desperately, "Please God. No! Not like this!!"

And in that moment, I did not know if I would live to see another day....

When I stood at the altar and took my wedding vows in 1983, one of the promises to which I committed myself was "...till death do us part." To be sure, not everyone makes that vow these days, for lots of reasons. But among the people that still do, and once did (like me) - not one of them utters those words thinking that the death that inevitably comes to all of us might be at the hand of their own spouse.

That's right: **My attacker was my husband** - the guy who promised to "...love, honor, and cherish..." me, *till death do us part.* No woman, standing at the altar, in *that* moment, ever imagines that the one they thought was their best friend could one day become the greatest threat to their survival. I certainly didn't.

And yet that's what happened to me. This is my story, and I'm telling it with the hope that it won't be your story too.

But if it already *is*, then I want you to know two things: *You deserve <u>better,</u>* and more importantly, ***there is a way out....***

Preface

Writing this book has been cathartic for me. I started sharing my story four years ago at universities in Mississippi. I shared a one-hour message called "Girl, You Deserve Better!" I met many women and some men who connected with me because we shared pasts with an Abuser. Their stories broke my heart, but they found, in me, a safe place to share. Many women told me that they had been abused in the past and had never told anyone about it. I encouraged them to start speaking about it....for two reasons. First of all, I know that those speeches helped me to heal. I didn't even know that I was still broken. And secondly, because I have learned that most Abusers are narcissists. They want to be seen as "good" people to outsiders. Therefore, the more light we can shed on those abuses that are happening behind closed doors and hold people accountable for their actions, the sooner it will stop. I am not naïve enough to think that we can stop it altogether. I do, however, think it will happen *less* often.

I needed to take the last step and put my story on paper so that others could learn from my mistakes. I did not write this book to gain sympathy or to bash my ex-husband. I wrote the book so that I could help the abused, *wherever* you are and *whoever* you are. My reach can go much further with a book. I just couldn't share enough in a one-hour speech to have the lasting effect I hope to achieve.

Sadly, abuse crosses all lines....gender, economics, countries, children, and animals. By sharing my story in such detail, I hope that others will come to know what I have learned in the last thirteen years, after I finally walked out the door, children in hand, and found a much better life. It was hard; I won't say that it was easy. I had to admit to myself that I stayed way too long and allowed my children to live in that environment as well. I don't beat myself up over that anymore...but I did for a while.

I intend to expand my reach on this subject by talking to sports teams with my message "Man Up!" I do not feel that athletes are all Abusers. Quite the opposite: I know that most are not. What I have come to realize is that young men need to hear my message and my story for three reasons. The first reason is because they are public figures. Young boys watch their sports heroes and will emulate their behavior. These prominent athletes have a responsibility to model the type of behavior that young boys and men should follow. The second reason I want to talk to young men is because they may not know the things that I have learned about abuse. You have to know the definition of abuse and what types of behaviors are abusive to identify it when you see it. If a young man had a father who was abusive he might be caught in the Chain of Abuse and not even realize it. And the third reason I need to talk to young athletes is to help them avoid making mistakes that may ruin their future career and their future happiness.

If I can save one life....this will have been a success.

One

If I was asked to come up with one word to describe my upbringing - it would be a challenge, honestly, to narrow it down. So many possibilities come to mind. And all of them would be true. But certainly, one of the *first* words I would choose, and one of the most comprehensive, would be **privileged**.

Now, as soon as I say that, I feel like I need to qualify it, because when you talk about "privilege" in today's context, all kinds of images and ideas pop into peoples' minds. And I get that. Let me tell you what *I mean* when I use that word. The kinds of privileges or advantages I am referencing have less to do with economics or social leverage than they do with relationships and family dynamics.

In short, I was (and still am) blessed to have wonderful parents who loved us and provided a stable and secure environment for me and my siblings. Were my parents perfect? Of course not. Would I have changed anything about my childhood? Certainly. But at the end of the day, the positives far outweighed the negatives. My parents loved each other - emotionally and behaviorally, even if not perfectly. Love was a noun *and* a verb in their relationship. It wasn't just something you *felt*. It was something you *did*, or refrained from doing, for the sake of the other.

And, in addition to providing/modeling a loving, stable home, my parents provided something else that would come into play in the midst of my marital breakdown - a point of reference. They gave me a way of recognizing what normal was and, more importantly, *what it wasn't*.

...with one significant qualification.

While my parents modeled so many wonderful things, most especially what it looks like for two people to love each other - and to *act* like it - there was one thing that was not helpful. Simply put, they really never let their kids see them argue and fight. Of course, they *did* fight. But we never saw or heard it. We were shielded from it, with the best of intentions, I'm sure.

However, good intentions don't always lead to good results. And so, the consequence for me (and my siblings) was that we didn't get to see that fighting and anger was a normal part of a *good* relationship. More importantly, we didn't get to see how it *could* be handled, how it was possible for two people who really did love each other to be deeply frustrated with each other at the same time. In short, I never saw a "good" fight.

That being said, I want to say again that I was (and remain) truly blessed and privileged to

have the parents that I have. They gave me a
point of reference that ultimately helped me to
see what was wrong with my marriage.

So, I truly *was* privileged. And right on
the heels of that let me also say: *I know not
everyone has that sort of privilege or advantage.*
The truth of that has been confirmed to me again
and again by the stories of so many women that
didn't have anything like that when they were
growing up.

And I guess that's just the thing. All of us
are scripted by our upbringings and bring all of
our experiences into our relationships - the good,
the bad and the in- between. The particulars of
our own experiences "set us up", so to speak, for
how we respond to the things that come our way
- including and especially within our
marriages/relationships. Often women will put
up with behaviors and situations that they
shouldn't - not because they are weak or
ignorant, but simply because their "normal"
predisposed them to see, and *not see* certain
realities. What they experienced in their family
of origin set them up for being in situations that,
although terribly cruel and unjust, still felt
strangely familiar and, as a result, didn't set off
the alarm bells that they *might* have - had they
grown up in different circumstances.

Birth-Order Blues

Another reality that shaped me a great
deal in my childhood - and which I carried into

my first marriage - was simply the fact that I am a first-born child (with my twin brother), with all of the attendant traits that typically go along with that.

Perhaps the main thing was the fact that I was, like so many first-borns, a *rule-keeper.* I was always very concerned about doing things the *"right" way* and, equally, *doing the "right" thing.* Those traits are not bad ones to have - in the abstract. The problem comes when doing the "right" thing is equated with doing the "expected" thing. In short, it all depends on whose dictionary you're using.

Sadly, and partially due to my first-born tendencies, I spent many, many years imprisoned by mere personal preferences that had been redefined and elevated to the level of absolute standards.

Still, there were other tendencies that showed up early on that would *not* contribute to my imprisonment, but would eventually help to set me *free* from it. For most of my junior high and high school years, I was the stereotypical nerdy, smart girl, complete with a Dorothy Hamill haircut and polyester pants (I know, what was I *thinking?).* For the most part, I was content to be in the background, breaking out ever-so-slightly here and there with my dance pursuits (ballet, dance team), clarinet lessons, and the obligatory membership in Girl Scouts. I wasn't unpopular, nor was I unhappy. Just vanilla: the sometimes-nameless girl whose brother was the Senior Class President.

Some of you will know *exactly* what I'm talking about.

But then graduation came and to the surprise of some (including myself a little bit), rather than join the hordes heading off to Louisiana State University (including my brother), I announced that I was doing something different. I was headed for the University of Southern Mississippi (USM), which I simply referred to as "Southern" (creating confusion in the minds of some, but that's another story).

The bottom line was this: I was at a point in my life where I wanted to meet new people, people who didn't know me and would have to get to know me on my terms, in the present, and not according to what they thought they knew about me from my life thus far. Going to USM, for me, was about getting a chance to try out "Christy 2.0". I didn't quite know what it would look like myself, but I was looking forward to it.

The College Years

So I hit the ground running and, almost immediately, started rolling out the upgrades, starting with my appearance. I let my hair grow long. I started playing sports - which I had never done. I was reinventing myself daily those first couple of years in college. I was *tired* of being the shy, smart girl who stood in the background. I decided that I could be smart and live a little. During that time my brother went through some big changes, spiritually, and made a special trip to tell me about his newfound faith. He loved me and wanted me to know what he had found. But that's not where I was at the time. He was trying to talk to me about life after death, but I couldn't hear him because I was too busy trying to figure out if there was life *before* death.

If that doesn't give you a good enough idea about what the transition was like for me, this will: I had my *second* beer in college. Literally. That may not sound surprising at first, but you have to understand that in 1979 the legal drinking age was 18, not 21. I had reached the legal drinking age in November of my senior year, so I had easy *and* legal access to alcohol. Nevertheless, as any high school kid could tell you then, all that was *legal* was not necessarily *permissible.* And so, I didn't dare drink in high school because I was terrified word would get back to my Dad somehow. Between his dental practice *and* his being on the local school board, as well as various service organizations, he knew thousands of people in town. The "six degrees of separation" principle might be in effect everywhere else in the world, but in Slidell, Louisiana, it was more like *two* degrees of separation between what was going on in town and my Dad's ears. Heading off to college brought the other four degrees back into the equation. And I took full advantage of that fact.

Another way I started branching out was in the area of relationships. During my first year of college I dated a USM cheerleader, which immediately moved me into social circles that were new for me. He was a sweet guy - a couple of years older and very cute. I remember thinking that he was almost *too* sweet. Looking back, I can hardly believe that I was so stupid as to have even *questioned* that, especially in light of what I have been through since. Hindsight can be brutal like that.

But, at the end of the day, you don't know what you don't know. And so, for whatever reason, and maybe even *against* reason, the spark just wasn't there, and I broke it off. In some ways, he was more like a *best* friend than a *boyfriend*. But I will never forget him. To this day, I still look back on that time and am sometimes baffled as to how I could have thought the way I did.

In the midst of everything else that was going on, there was another event that proved to be the main turning point in the developing plotline for me: I became a little sister for a fraternity. And it was there that I met the man who would become my first husband - and the other main character in this story. We'll call him "Paul".

Now, some of you will not be familiar with this at all, but I'm old enough to remember the TV show "Dragnet" - one of the early crime dramas. And it was truly groundbreaking (at least back then it was) because its storylines were based on real events. As a result, at the beginning of the show, as they were setting up the story, they used this now iconic phrase to remind the viewers that, although the story itself was true, "...the names have been changed to protect the innocent."

I say all of that to say *this*: for the purposes of my story, we're changing his name. But it has nothing to do with innocence. *Nothing.*

So, I met Paul and our first date was the Homecoming game in the fall of my sophomore year. And, as first impressions go, I have to say it was a good start. All the things I had seen growing up - values and practices that my Dad had taught and modeled - things that were "normal" for me were all there. Doors were opened, chairs pulled out, etc. In short, he treated me like a lady, like someone who mattered.

As for himself, he was polite and respectful of others. "Yes Sirs" and "Yes Ma'ams" showed up at all the appropriate places. He was well dressed, drove a nice car, and he was a good dancer. As a result, I thought that I had found a good man....one that would always treat me right. There was certainly nothing there - at the time - that should have caused me to think otherwise.

Another thing that caught my attention early on was that, in addition to everything else, he had all the earmarks of being a successful person - someone who was going *somewhere*. In other words, there was this sense that I had found a guy who, along with everything else, could offer some assurances of financial security, something that was an important factor for me at the time.

To be sure, I grew up in a comfortable home and came from a context where I never lacked anything I needed. At the same time, I had a Dad who believed that his kids needed to learn how to "stand on their own two feet" - in lots of ways, including financially. Translation: Any money I had in college was money *I made*. And it wasn't much. That was a new situation for me and so the attraction of a man who looked like he could provide, among other things, *financial* stability was pretty strong and, as I now see much more clearly, much stronger than it should have been.

And so, we continued to date and, as we neared the end of our time at college, Paul, in his Senior year, became the President of his fraternity and I, one year behind him, became the President of my sorority (Delta Gamma) - and it felt like something right out of a 1950's Mickey Rooney movie. We were the couple that would go out into the world and do something remarkable. Looking back, the naiveté was rich, but in the moment, it just felt like this was how the world was supposed to be. How could we *not* succeed?

But it wasn't *all* sunshine and roses. There were some early behaviors and incidents that, at the time, and in the wake of everything else that was going on, did not seem significant, and did not suggest that anything terrible was on the horizon. Looking back, I see now that they were early warning signs. In my own defense, however, I would say it wasn't because I was stupid or wasn't paying attention. I just didn't have the perspective yet to see them for what they were.

For example, Paul started this habit of either walking me or driving me to class. And then, when my class was over, he would be there waiting for me. At the time I just thought he was being sweet. I saw his actions as indicators of care and attentiveness, nothing more. And I'm not saying there was nothing of that in them. But over time, and as the "data" of my experiences started to mount up, I came to view his actions very differently. What I thought was kindness was really more about control. What I thought was motivated by care for me was, as I came to see all too clearly, largely about self-interest and managing the perceptions of others.

The other things that started showing up in those early years, and which I didn't realize was the leading edge of a much bigger storm, were his occasional displays of anger. Everybody gets angry, I know. But what started to show up was *anger that was disproportional to whatever it was that precipitated it.* Two incidents in particular come to mind in those early years.

The first one happened when we were studying at the fraternity house. He was reading a textbook and I could see that he was starting to get frustrated. He started muttering words under his breath, and then he started swearing, and he became more and more vocal and demonstrative. Finally, in a fit of rage he grabbed his notebook and his textbook - and he ripped them both to shreds and tossed them out into the hall. I tried to calm him down, but he was very angry and wouldn't have any of it. To be fair, on that particular occasion, he did not direct his anger at me, but I still left. He did call me later and apologize.

That was the first time I saw his temper. In a matter of minutes, he went from being fine to being out-of-control and over-the-top angry and violent. That's why I left. Because it was scary and I had never seen him exhibit that type of behavior before..... and I just didn't know how to handle it. After some time had passed I managed to convince myself that this was NOT his "normal" nature and that he was *just* stressed out and worried about getting a good grade in his class. All was good, as far as I could see.

The second incident took place when we were at a party in the fraternity house. It was late at night. Everyone was drinking beer and talking in the living room, some were watching TV, and others were dancing in the party room. I was dancing with Paul, and a guy that was dancing beside me - and was very drunk - kept bumping into me. This happened a couple of times and then Paul, with no warning, just lost his temper and with one punch, knocked the guy out cold. I was immediately shocked but quickly found a way to dismiss his behavior - rationalizing that he wasn't being aggressive, he was being *heroic*. His actions weren't inappropriate - they were noble. After all, he had "saved" me from a drunk.

Yeah, that's what it was. *Absolutely*.

Years later, when I was more capable of seeing these things for what they *really* were, I realized that Paul's actions were, of course, not heroic at all. Asking the drunk to move away or just removing ourselves from the dance floor would have been a much better way to handle the situation. That whole matter could have been approached a dozen different ways, with very different outcomes. But Paul's dysfunctionality and (as I came to see later) his limited people skills made him like a man who, because the only tool in his toolbox is a hammer, treats everything like a nail.

But, again, I found a way to take these things in stride and, aided by my youthful idealism, I continued to believe that I had found a good man. And so, while on a ski trip later that year with his family, he stopped in the middle of a slope, knelt down, pulled a ring out of his jacket and asked me to marry him. I immediately said

"Yes". I was sure I knew what I was doing. I was sure it was the *right* thing to do.

And yet, the truth is, just like every other person that says "yes" to that question, *I had no earthly idea what I was signing up for.*

<u>Two</u>

Paul and I both graduated in May of 1983. Even though he was a year ahead of me, he stayed in school another two semesters to earn his Masters in Business Administration while I finished up my Bachelor of Science in Business, with an emphasis in Accounting. I think, at the time, we both felt a strong sense of accomplishment and were hopeful about "the future". We weren't sure *where* we were going, but wherever it was, we were pretty confident that things would work out.

After graduation, I immediately started sending out letters to companies that had open accounting positions and, while I waited for an interview, I worked as a teller at a bank in my hometown of Slidell. As for Paul, his job search took him farther afield, including (for reasons I can no longer recall) California, of all places. To be sure, I wasn't totally opposed to that as a possibility, but I still found myself looking at places a little closer to home - like Dallas. I wasn't looking for anything exotic and far away, just bigger, with more opportunities - something that would take me beyond my small-town roots (apologies to John Cougar Mellencamp).

As it turned out, Paul's west coast excursion didn't result in any job offers -

partially because - truth be known - I don't think job hunting was his main concern when he was there. Meanwhile, I was back at home, and receiving the first of what would eventually become a significant number of "Dear John" letters. You know the drill I'm sure. They all start out so well - "Thank you so much for your application" - and then they insert that *wretched* word: BUT. From there it's all downhill and, no matter how many positive things they say, it still feels like a kick in the gut.

However, I persisted in applying and one day I got a promising call. It was the Human Resource Director at Hunt Petroleum. He told me that they did not have an accounting position open at that point in time, but he would still like to talk to me "whenever I was in Dallas" - just in case one did come up in the near future. I thanked him for his call and hung up the phone. I was so excited that I could hardly think about anything else that day. The next morning, I decided I couldn't sit around and wait anymore, so I took action. Call it a "whim", call it "intuition" - call it what you want - but I felt compelled to do *something*. So, I got the HR Director on the phone once again and announced that I would be in Dallas on the following Wednesday and asked if he would be available. He said he would and we made an appointment right then and there.

The following Wednesday I took the red eye to Dallas and by 10 A.M. was sitting across from him in an interview. At the end of our meeting he asked me who else I would be interviewing with while I was in Dallas. I told him that I didn't have any other interviews lined up and was flying back home that night. He couldn't believe it and actually felt bad about the fact that I had spent the money and time to come to Dallas - for one interview - and, beyond that, with a company that wasn't even hiring to positions in my field! I assured him that it was okay and told him that I didn't feel at all bad about making the trip because I *wanted* to meet him, and to get to know a little more about the Company and, quite honestly, make sure he met me so that, when a position *did* open up he would think of me first. I think that made him feel better about the whole thing and he ended up taking me to lunch and then made sure I had transportation to the airport.

As I left, I really didn't know what sort of impression I was leaving him with. Did I come across as too desperate? I honestly couldn't say. Thankfully I didn't have to wait long. Two weeks later he called to tell me that, even though there were no positions, the company had decided to *create* a position for me. He said they were impressed with my initiative at such a young age. I was so excited!

And so, it was a very encouraging start for me, personally. I felt good about who I was. I liked myself. The strange thing is, as I look back on that time, to this very day I wonder at how *that* young woman, who had started out with so much confidence, and initiative and just plain *gumption* - how could someone like *that* turn into this frightened, submissive and tolerant-to-a-fault wife that I would become? The answer...... *gradually.*

How "Gradually" Started

To no one's surprise, Paul and I married in August of 1983, right before the move to Dallas. He still hadn't found a job, but again, our confidence was pretty high and we both felt certain that he would soon be gainfully employed and, as it turned out, he *was*, taking a job with a company that was located just across the street from my own office.

And so that was it: we were finally established - the fairy tale (or so I thought) was launched. School was over, we had gotten married, we had moved to the big city, and we both had good paying jobs. We were living the dream, and our futures were assured and secured. As I look back on that now, I cannot believe how naive some of my early perspectives were. But, as I said before, you don't know what you don't know. As far as I was concerned, life was going to be good and we were doing all the "right" things to make it so (#OldestChildSyndrome).

It didn't take long, however, before cracks started to appear in the foundation.

For starters, I learned very quickly that there were only two ways to do everything. There was Paul's way of doing it (the "right" way), and then there was any *other* way of doing the same thing - which included mine. That was "the wrong way". There were no other options.

Now, it would have been one thing if Paul's opinions on how everything should be done were just that: *opinions.* But they weren't presented as opinions. They were standards. And there was no tolerance for deviation from those standards, as I quickly learned. And perhaps if he had only acted that way about things *occasionally* I could have handled it better. I'm certainly not immune to doing the same thing sometimes. **But that was just it** - it wasn't that he acted like this *rarely*. In those early months together, he did it all the time. And further, his opinions weren't confined to one or two areas. He had opinions (read: "Iron Clad Rules") about *everything.*

As I look back, I am sometimes amazed and surprised that this aspect of his person/character escaped my notice when we were just dating. Part of the reason, I think, is that it wasn't as prevalent in the early days as it later became. Another reason was probably that it was there, and I just didn't *want* to see it.

However, I think the biggest reason I didn't see it early on was because we weren't living together at the time and, as a result, I only had to deal with it relatively infrequently and - by the same token - he didn't have as many occasions to correct me. In other words, in those circumstances, there wasn't enough of a signature for it to show up on the radar.

Whatever the reason, I had never seen this side of him before. Now we were together all the time. Accordingly, I started receiving instructions on the right and wrong way to do <u>everything</u> - how to put toilet paper on the holder correctly, how to load the forks in the dishwasher, how to separate the utensils into their proper places, how to wash clothes, how to properly fold a shirt, pants, etc. There was almost no area of my life in which I was not eventually instructed. Apparently, I had spent my entire life doing almost everything the wrong way. And now I was living with a man whose personal opinions, as I've previously noted, had been raised to the level of absolute standards.

But I was young, and my attendant optimism was still pretty resilient. And so, for the sake of "peace", I just put up with it. I wasn't a complete doormat, mind you; he got some pushback from me at different times. But the relentlessness of the situation and his increasing agitation and anger, over time, made pushing back seem less and less like a good or wise idea.

Not surprisingly, I cried a lot that first year. This behavior pattern that seemed to have come out of nowhere felt more and more oppressive. It wasn't like this right away, but in time it became this growing "presence" that always seemed to be lurking somewhere in the room. Sadly, it was never very far away. I began to see that I had married a very controlling person who felt it was his duty to "fix me" in areas where I had never realized I was "broken".

Not having any preparation for this, I decided that, although I didn't like it, I had to learn to make the best of it. Secretly, I think I still held out hope that it wouldn't always be this way - that he would relax and not be so exacting all the time.

As an aside to that, my brother asked me once why I didn't reach out to anyone during that time of my life. He wasn't being judgmental - just curious. After reflecting on that, I told him that there were at least three reasons. The first one was pride, plain and simple. Things had not gotten to any terrible stage yet in our relationship, but there was enough going on for me to wonder if I had made a huge mistake marrying Paul. Frankly, I didn't want to admit that to anyone. It was embarrassing. A second reason was isolation. I was living in a new place, without many friends yet and not much family support that was immediately available. The third reason was - again - that I didn't know what I didn't know. Maybe what I was going through was just an "adjustment" - I would say to myself. Maybe this was normal, and everybody dealt with this at some level.

And, in reality, what helped me to convince myself, for quite some time, that maybe it *was* normal, is the fact that once we got through those early months, the corrections and instructions *did* become less frequent. However, the reasons for that were not a reflection of changed behavior on Paul's part. He remained as exacting and critical as ever. It was two other factors that accounted for the changed frequency. One of them was the simple fact that, when we first began living together, the "set" of things that I needed to be instructed on was much larger. It was everything. I was like a new "employee" that has to be shown how to do everything at the office. But once I got through the initial round of instructions - once Paul "broke me in" - the sessions only took place as new things happened, or circumstances changed or, God forbid, I forgot a previous instruction and did it wrong - AGAIN.

Which then leads to the other factor: I *adjusted.* I decided/learned, rightly or wrongly, that it was better to just go with the flow and do things "his" way even when I felt that there was often a better, or at least equally good alternative way to do things. Again, I decided to *keep the peace.*

But whatever "peace" I felt I was gaining by making those choices, there were huge *losses* and trade-offs that went with it. In other words, there was a big, although not that easily recognized, price tag attached to that alleged peace: the price tag of internal turmoil, the price tag of eroding self-respect, the price tag of declining hopes for the future of my marriage - to name just a few of the mounting deficits. In short, fairly early on in my marriage, *I had this growing suspicion that the man I had promised to spend the rest of my life with was not going to love me for who I was, but rather, for how I performed.*

All my life I had heard people talking about the "honeymoon being over". I just didn't realize it would be over so quickly.

Blindsided

Before I tell you *exactly* how the honeymoon ended, let me set up the story. Paul had always been a very fit person. It mattered a lot to him. As for me, while I wasn't in bad shape, or anything like it, going to the gym had never really been my "thing." But it was important to Paul and so, when we were in college, I started to go with him on his workouts. Eventually I came to enjoy it for my own reasons.

But, as I look back on it now, I see it, as yet another way Paul wanted to control me. He was terrified that I might get fat and he had a plan to keep that from happening. In other words, my being in shape was more about him and his satisfaction and what people might think about him than it was about me and my health and well-being. While that sad reality was not lost on me, I had found, nevertheless, that working out was a good thing and having regular physical exercise was a great way to process some of the growing stress that I felt over my marital situation.

And so, on one particular Saturday, we decided to take advantage of the especially beautiful weather to get some exercise. We headed out on the streets of Dallas. I was riding his 10-speed bike and he was jogging along at a pretty good clip beside me. After I had been riding for a little bit, I reached down to shift gears and, as soon as I did, something got jammed and the chain came off.

Well, from what happened next, you would have thought I had just deliberately driven a BMW into a tree. Like a bolt of lightning coming from a seemingly cloudless sky, Paul became *instantly* furious in a way, and with an intensity, that completely caught me off guard and which was totally disproportional to what allegedly had set it off. It was an effect in search of a cause.

And so, for the next few minutes, he just went *off* - swearing at me, calling me "stupid", belittling me and just plain shaming me for shifting the gears "wrong" and "messing up the chain". And so, he stood over me, dog-cussing me and screaming instructions for how to get the chain back on. This went on for several minutes and, in the end, I just wasn't able to get the chain back on, which only made him angrier.

And so, out of sheer spite, and instead of fixing it himself, he decided I needed to learn a lesson. He then "punished" me by ordering me to pick up the bike - which I dutifully did - and I carried it all the way home, while he walked and fumed beside me. Some of you reading this will think, "There is *no way* I would have done that." And I won't argue with you. But for many women reading this, who have been in abusive situations, you will not be surprised at my doing that. Because you've done similar things that, at the time, you didn't resist, and which now causes you to wonder, "What was wrong with me? Why did I do that?"

Don't beat yourself up, please. You are not alone.

Sadly, that was only the first of *many, many* similar encounters. But because it WAS the first one of that magnitude - it just took my breath away. I was completely blindsided by this rage that showed up out of *nowhere.* And so, *as* I struggled to lug this bike all the way to our apartment, my head was filled with a whirlwind of emotions - confusion, shame, embarrassment, anger, fear - and a dozen other things. Questions were racing through my mind as I tried to figure out what had gone wrong, or what it was that I had done that had resulted in this otherwise unexplainable outburst.

As we walked along, the silence was palpable between us. Eventually we made it back and I don't think I spoke to him for the rest of the day. It wasn't until the next day, late in the afternoon, that he finally managed to deliver an apology that was more strategic than it was remorseful. He had no clue how badly he had made me feel over such a small thing. And he didn't bother to ask.

He said he was sorry, checked the box, and moved on to the next task.

Growing Evidence

The bike riding episode, for me, was the first clear signal that maybe things *weren't* as normal as I desperately wanted to believe. And, as I have already suggested, that incident all by itself, while shocking, would not necessarily have caused me to begin wondering. Was there something dysfunctional going on or was this an isolated incident?

But, again, <u>that's just the thing</u>: It *wasn't* isolated. To be sure, while Paul's corrections and instructions weren't taking place as *often* as they did at first - they *were* still happening with great *regularity*. More disturbingly, as the bike incident showed so clearly, they were happening with *increasingly unjustifiable levels of emotion*. Corrections and frustrations that were previously delivered in a normal tone of voice were now routinely being delivered with all manner of swearing and with the clear intent of being hurtful.

Alongside the bike episode, there was another development that was taking place. And maybe development is not quite the right word - but there was something that was starting to show up - a detectable pattern or reality about Paul that would eventually be a major contributing factor in the unraveling of our marriage - and it had do with Paul's *work*.

While Paul had managed to find gainful employment when we were in Dallas, he was clearly not happy with his work. He was constantly complaining about the job and made a point of letting me know how bored he was doing it. He started looking for other options. Finally, his restlessness about the whole thing came to a head and, to my great surprise, he announced that what he *really* wanted to do was join the military.

When he made that announcement, I
honestly didn't know what to think. On the one
hand, I loved my job and really enjoyed living in
Dallas. On the other hand, I still loved my
husband - even though I was increasingly hurt
and confused by his actions - and I knew, or at
least hoped, that our life together might get
better if my husband was happy with his job. So,
I encouraged him to pursue the career that he
thought would make him happy. In a very short
time he was on his way to finding out whether he
might be accepted in the Naval Aviation
program. And, for a time at least, he did seem
happier once we made that decision.

Goodbye Dallas, Hello Pensacola

As Paul was hoping, he was selected to
attend Aviation Officer Candidate School (AOCS).
Think: "An Officer and a Gentleman" and you've
got a good idea what sort of life we had
transitioned to. And so, while he went through
the program and lived in the barracks, I moved
back home to stay with my Mom and Dad until
Paul graduated. I gave up a job I loved and had
accepted a very different sort of life, but I still felt
it was the right thing for me to do at the time.
Trying to make the most of the time while Paul
went through the twelve-week program, I kept
my feet on the ground and my head in the books,
studying for my CPA (Certified Public
Accountant) exam. It was a difficult time, to say
the least. I was back home at the age of 23 and
without a job....which had never happened to me

since the age of 15. However, I consoled myself, as much as I could, with the thought that at least I was doing something to move my career forward.

Back in Pensacola, Paul had been elected "President" of his AOCS class and, of course, he loved it. No doubt, part of his popularity came from the fact that, contrary to the stereotypes, he simply was not afraid of the stereotypical "Screaming Drill Sergeant" and, in fact, thought it was funny when others *were*. Now, it may not be meaningful at all, and I wouldn't pretend to be a psychologist, but I have certainly wondered at times about that. Maybe it is significant that a man with serious anger issues felt completely comfortable in a testosterone-driven context that traffics in *anger* and *rage*. Was there something I *missed*?

It was two weeks before graduation and Paul called to tell me to schedule movers for the next weekend. I did as he asked and the next weekend I was in Pensacola with the movers, unpacking boxes and getting our new home set up. It was a big apartment with large rooms, high ceilings, wooden floors, arched entry ways and a beautiful screened porch under majestic oak trees. We were in base housing, and this was so much better than I had expected! I had even brought the top of our wedding cake because we would be celebrating our first anniversary in our new home. Paul was far enough into the program that he had "leave" that weekend. He showed up late that Friday afternoon. After making up for some lost time, we went to the grocery store to get what we needed to make a romantic dinner. I had not seen Paul for several weeks and was looking forward to our evening together. We only needed a few things, so I picked up one of the small hand-held baskets as we entered the Commissary. When we got to the check-out stand I just put the basket up on the conveyer belt. Within seconds Paul's whole attitude changed. He became quiet and I could see that his jaw was clenched. The cashier removed the items from the basket, rang them up and transferred them to plastic bags. I paid, grabbed the bags and walked out. Paul was ahead of me - obviously mad about something - and was walking quickly to the car. Before we got into the car, because he couldn't hold it in any longer, he started screaming at me about what an idiot I was. "Nobody puts the basket on the conveyer belt!", he screamed. He called me names and made me feel so embarrassed. I could not understand what had caused this sudden outburst. We had not seen each other for weeks and all I did was put a basket on a conveyer belt. Apparently, that was a mortal sin.

When we got back to the apartment I went for a walk and was gone for a very long time. When I came back I told him how upset I was and how I didn't appreciate him screaming at me over such a small thing. (What I should have said, in hindsight, is that he should never scream at me about ANYTHING!) He did apologize, but it ruined the celebration I had thought we would be having.

Upon graduating from the AOCS program, Paul was told he would need to drive 27 miles to Milton, Florida, each day to do his flight training. This was too far for him to drive, so we went to Milton and tried to find a place to live. There was not much to offer in Milton. I tried to reason with him that it was only a 27-mile drive, but Paul told me that it would be too much with the stress of flight school. So....he got us transferred to Corpus Christi, Texas, and off we went again.

Once again, I had to start interviewing for a job, but at this point I was feeling a little more confident. After all, I was an Honors Graduate in Accounting, I told myself. I had some accounting experience as well. How hard could it be? As it turns out, very hard. No one would hire me because they knew my husband was in training at the Navy base and we would only be there six months to a year.

Nevertheless, I persisted, and eventually landed a job as the cashier at a car wash during the day and the bookkeeper for the business at night. I was also studying to finish the CPA exam. I had passed three of the four parts and just had to finish the last one.

It was during this season of our life that another pretty revealing incident took place. Not long after we had moved to Corpus, Paul met a man who owned several old Corvettes. For a kid who had grown up working on vintage cars, it was a dream scenario and, inevitably, we ended up purchasing one of the Corvettes and proceeding to rebuild the engine. In reality, Paul was building the engine and I was his personal assistant, but I have to say, in spite of all the drama around it, I actually started to get into it a little bit.

At any rate, the Corvette was parked in a storage unit across the street from our apartment. Summertime in Corpus Christi is NOT the ideal time to work on a car - at least not during the day - so we ended up working on the car at night, when the conditions were a little more bearable.

We were close to finishing the engine. We only had to put on the carburetor for it to be completed. I was helping to screw the wing nuts on and, somehow, I managed to drop one down into the engine. It happens, right? Not in Paul's universe. In an almost exact duplication of the bike incident - Paul once again *lost his mind*. With a rage that was completely uncalled for, he screamed and cussed and proceeded to make sure I knew how completely worthless I was as a human being. And then, once he had finished berating me he angrily handed me a flashlight and once more felt it was his duty to "punish" me for being so *stupid* as to drop something. And so, while he could have easily figured out a way to suspend the flashlight above the engine so he could see, he instead made me stand there for at least two hours while he took pieces of the engine off, in order to locate the missing wing nut. It was humiliating and completely uncalled for. But once more, I dutifully stood there and put up with it, not daring to move, and terrified the entire time that I might do something else to set him off. What was the great "sin" I had committed to deserve all of this?

I dropped something. I was human. *How dare I?*

A few months later Paul received the disappointing news that, because he had displayed some vertigo-like symptoms when performing certain high G-force maneuvers, he would not be allowed to complete the pilot training, although he *could* still continue in the program as a Navigator. To borrow from "Top Gun" - he couldn't be "Maverick" - but he could still be "Goose".

At first, he seemed alright with this and wanted to continue, even though it wasn't exactly what he had signed up for. However, once he got the news that he would have to be on a waiting list to get into the Navigator aspect of the program the whole thing seemed less attractive to him. And when he was told that while he was waiting he would be assigned to an aircraft carrier near China for six months - that tipped the scale in his mind. Within a very short amount of time he received an honorable discharge and we were out of the Navy and on our way to Houston, where his sister was living.

Houston....We Have a Problem

I found a job quickly in Houston, working with a local accounting firm that specialized in construction audits. This was in spite of the fact that my resume, at that point, depicted me as a person who never stayed at a job for more than a year (one of the liabilities of living with a man who was vocationally homeless). As it would turn out (again) I would not keep *this* job for much more than a year either. But I didn't know that at the time and did enjoy the fact that I was learning new things and had a chance to work with one of the partners on several of the audits, who quickly took the top spot on my list of "favorite bosses".

Once again, while I had landed a job very quickly, *Paul struggled to find work that he was happy with*. Eventually he took a job at a local gym, but that soon became a source of great frustration and irritation for him - to my dismay. And so, in our short tenure together as husband and wife, Paul's job history to this point looked like this:

1) Graduates from college - looks for work in California - no result

2) Takes a job with an oil and gas company in Dallas - the job was "boring and frustrating"

3) Out of the blue, declares he wants to be a Navy Pilot - we make the move - but he can't stay in the program as a Pilot, although he is still eligible to be a Navigator. When he is told that he will have to be on a waiting list and be deployed on a ship until then - he decides to leave.

4) We move to Houston - he can't find the job he wants - settles for a job working at a gym - finds the job frustrating and irritating.

Again, it was still fairly early in the marriage, but there was a pattern of restlessness, dissatisfaction, boredom, and frustration that was becoming more and more evident. I don't think I saw it as clearly *then* as I do now - but it was certainly there.

And so, it was, in the midst of yet another frustrating work situation for Paul, there was another "incident" that, when added to the other things that had happened, *also* began looking more and more like a pattern. A very *disturbing* one.

I was making my commute home one day
- one and a half hours each direction, mind you -
when I decided to pull into a drive-through
before getting onto the interstate to get a soft
drink for the long drive home. I don't remember
exactly what month and day it was, but I
remember it was winter. As I approached the
drive-through window I lowered the electric
window, paid for my drink, grabbed it, and began
pulling out. As I did, I hit the button to close the
window - and nothing happened. It was stuck
and nothing I did could make it go up.

Not having any other option at the time, I
gritted my teeth and headed out on the 90-
minute drive home. It was absolutely *freezing*
the entire way and my car's heater just couldn't
keep up. Eventually, I pulled into the driveway
and, once inside, I told Paul what had happened
with the window.

Once again, Paul went *ballistic*. Never
mind that there wasn't a thing I did wrong.
Never mind that it would have happened on his
watch if he had been driving the car. None of
that mattered to him. There was no reasoning
with him. It was *my fault* because I *insanely -
stupidly* - tried to use the window. He tried to
argue that if I hadn't gone through the drive-
through, this would never have happened. "Why
did you have to go through the drive-through?"
he shouted.

He continued to berate me for my stupidity and worked himself into a senseless, juvenile fit of rage. And in the midst of all that, he suddenly turned and *punched his fist right through the garage wall.*

I had seen him angry before - but I had never seen *this* kind of angry. Once again, all kinds of emotions and questions were racing through my mind in the aftermath of all that. "Who is this man?" I wondered. "What is going on here? Where is all this fury coming from?"

I had no answers. Frightened, angry, confused and humiliated - I walked away.

The next day, just as with the previous incidents, a half-hearted apology was issued. And then, once that was over with, once the incantation had been uttered and the magic words spoken, everything was supposed to be "all good". The unspoken, but painfully clear expectation was that I needed to just pick myself up and keep going, and not dwell on what was now in the past.

"Just move along...... Nothing to see here."

———————————————

At some point after all that, Paul started talking about moving back home to Mississippi. Although I was not opposed to that idea, I told him that I didn't want to give up my good job and make *another* move unless he had a job *before* we left. So, he started looking for a job in Mississippi. As it turned out, his uncle owned a funeral home in Jackson and - taking yet another surprising "career" turn - the next thing I knew we were on our way to Mississippi where Paul would begin his new job - as a *funeral director.* The pattern of restlessness for Paul to find a vocational "home" became increasingly obvious with every move.

Nevertheless, I was compliant and got back in line, still holding on to the fading hope that eventually my husband would find something and settle down. With the decision made, Paul quickly found us a little house, not far from the funeral home, and off we went. *Again.* After only 18 months in Houston, we were packing another moving truck.

Maybe things would be better in Mississippi.

Maybe...

Three

Paul and I had talked about children when we were dating, but the subject did not come up much after we were married. To be sure, I wanted children, and I thought he did too, but when we were in college we had decided not to start a family until we were both employed. And, while we both *had been* employed up to this point, the reality is that there was probably just too much going on, too many moving parts and too little sense of being "settled" for it to seem like a sensible discussion to pick up.

It was 1987; we had been married four years. Now we were in Jackson, Mississippi, we were both employed - again - and I was feeling pretty settled in our new home. It was very modest, but it worked. Paul had found the house, and even though it was not what I wanted, I did not complain. I proceeded to do my best to make it better by ripping out old wallpaper and decorating on a budget. I was still working out in the gym, I was young, and I was healthy.

AND.... I was *pregnant*.

Of course, we hadn't *planned* this pregnancy but then again - how many millions of people have said *that?* It just "happened" - as it does - and now I was expecting, and *Paul didn't know yet*. And he didn't know because I wasn't sure what his reaction would be. After all, we *still* hadn't picked up the family discussion - despite the fact that we were now more settled than we had ever been. We hadn't discussed whether or not this was the right time to start a family, and I just had no confidence that this news would be well-received by him.

On the day that the pregnancy was confirmed by my doctor, Paul surprised me and brought home an armoire that he had bought from his Uncle. I had been complaining about not having enough storage space in this small, older home and, in response and unknown to me, Paul had been asking around and came up with a solution to our storage issues - which I have to admit was helpful. And so, although it was extremely heavy, and I probably shouldn't have been doing it, I helped him move it inside. I think it was perhaps that *gesture* on his part that gave me the courage to go ahead and tell him I was pregnant. And so, tentatively, I broke the news to him and - to my surprise - he was *happy*, which helped me - finally - to actually enjoy the news myself.

At this point, I just want to say that I don't have any difficulty looking back on my marriage and seeing things that were good and nice and right, at times, about Paul - like when he went out and found us an armoire. None of us are one-dimensional beings that are either complete angels or utterly demonic. We're all a mixed bag - and that mix is not the same for any two people.

That being said, things were done and said to me, and my children, that ought never be done to anyone - and can never be justified. And yet I can tell *that* story without having to resort to factual distortions and without reducing Paul to a one-dimensional psychopath utterly devoid of any decency or humanity. People are more complex than that.

Indeed, that is part of the reason women - like me - can find themselves in the *midst* of these situations. It's not as if we completely lose our minds one day and go out and marry men who are *obviously* complete monsters - and anybody can see that. No, we meet people who are capable of good and evil, who have virtues and deep flaws, who are multi-dimensional. And as we are getting to know them, we see enough good things that convince us that there is a believable future with a certain guy and we take the plunge. The problem is not that we discover one day that our partner, like us, is flawed. The problem is when we discover that our partner doesn't see the flaws that are clearly there, has no interest in addressing them, is not bothered that they are hurtful and destructive to us and our families, and is *unwilling to change*.

And so, again, Paul surprised me when he was happy to learn of my being pregnant. And I have no difficulty saying, even today, that it was a nice, although brief, moment in our marriage.

Three months after "the reveal" I went for a regular visit to my OB-GYN, and the doctor did a routine ultrasound to check on the baby. Prior to that visit I had not been feeling well, but without any previous experience to draw on, I had convinced myself that this was probably how *all* pregnant women felt.

I was wrong. The doctor completed the ultrasound, not saying much, until he delivered the heart-breaking news that my fetus, my son, had died in my womb. While I was still trying to cope with the enormity of what he had said, he quickly drew up orders for me to go to Woman's Hospital so that he could perform a D & C that same day.

I was utterly devastated. It had only been three months, but I had grown to love my as-yet-unmet child - and now I was being told that I had a "missed abortion", i.e., that my body "should" have naturally dispelled the dead fetus but didn't somehow. I knew what they meant, but the language of "should" and "abortion" combined with the death of my child in the same sentence was terribly upsetting to me. This was my *baby* they were talking about - a baby I *wanted and loved.* And even though they were talking about my body *performing a function* (or not, as the case was) and not me *making a choice* - it still was, in my judgment, a poor way to describe what "should" have happened. It wasn't anything I wanted, with or without the cooperation of my body. And yet it was over now, and I had to deal with it. And so, broken-hearted and hurting, I submitted to the horrid procedure.

Afterwards I was taken home and for several days I laid in my bed crying. I thought I might never be able to have a baby. And I did what many other women have done in that situation - I began to blame myself. I speculated that perhaps it was the moving of the armoire that led to the terrible disaster. The truth is I don't know - and never will. But whatever the connection was - or wasn't - one thing was clear to me: I should never have been in a situation where I was so fearful of my husband's temper that it kept me from speaking up when I felt that I should, especially when my own child's well-being was at stake.

At the risk of boorish redundancy let me say it again: I'm not saying there was a definite connection between me moving the armoire and losing my baby. *The problem was that I didn't feel free or safe to even break the news and raise the question.* It would not be the last time I would feel similarly constrained. But I eventually found the strength to break the pattern. To this day, I still wonder about all of that, but I know I will see my son again. And that will be a very good day.

Three months later, and although still deeply sad about my loss, I became pregnant again. And, this time, it was a healthy pregnancy. It didn't "replace" my loss - which is a ridiculous notion - but it did renew my hopes, and so my precious son was born in January 1988. I was 27 years old, and I adored him from the moment I saw him. I told myself that now I had the happiness I had been searching for....a child of my own who would love me unconditionally, as I would love him. I embraced being a mother with all my heart and soul.

Even so, and in spite of being absolutely in *love* with my baby boy, I had to be back at work just six weeks later, diving into a full-blown tax season. It wasn't my first preference, I can tell you. But the reality then - and which *remained* a reality for the remainder of my marriage - is that I was the main breadwinner in our family. It hurt my heart, but I knew I had to keep working. To be honest, I did/do *like* my work....most days....but it was truly hard to be away from my child, especially when he was very young. It was incredibly difficult to take my son to daycare each day and leave him with others to spend those precious hours. I cried a lot those first few weeks. But in the end, like it or not, I did what I had to do, working 60-hour work weeks for the next six weeks until the end of tax season. It was physically AND emotionally exhausting.

To make matters worse, not only was I working crazy hours, I was still expected to be the one to get up every night, in the middle of the night, to take care of <u>our</u> son - singlehandedly. It wasn't the fact that my son needed care that was the issue. It was the *attitude* and *assumption* that it was my responsibility - and mine alone - no matter how exhausted I felt. That was what got to me. Whatever Paul and I had, it wasn't anything approaching a *partnership*.

I remember one night when my son woke up screaming for his bottle. There was no corner or room in that small house that you could not hear him crying. I decided to "pretend" that I was in a deep sleep, hoping that Paul would finally help out. I was not breastfeeding our son at this point, so my participation in the nightly feedings was not always necessary. There wasn't a snowflake's chance of that happening as Paul had decided to "pretend" as well. I knew he was awake. There was no way he could not hear what was going on. But he wasn't about to make a move. I was livid as I rolled over and pushed him and said "I *know* you hear your son. You're not fooling anybody....." It was clear to me that I was going to do the bulk of the child-rearing all on my own. I didn't know it at the time, but the years of carrying the bulk of the parenting responsibilities, on top of my full-time job outside of the home, would take its toll on me. To this day, I am convinced that I shaved unknown years off my life - all because my "partner" didn't care enough to take his share of the responsibility for raising and caring for our children.

We remained in Jackson for a total of about 2 ½ years, but Paul's work with his Uncle in the funeral business lasted only about a year. Indeed, he had only been at it for a couple of months when his frustration and restlessness started to rear its ugly head once again. And, true to the pattern that was becoming clearer and clearer to me, when Paul was frustrated with his work, the rest of us ended up paying a price for it.

And so, near the end of his time working at the funeral parlor we experienced yet another completely inexcusable and downright frightening example of Paul's behavioral pattern

The incident happened on a Saturday when he had been scheduled to work and, as he was unable to go out and get anything to eat, he called and asked me to bring him some lunch. So, I made him one of his favorite meals - a baked open-faced ham and cheese sandwich. After it was heated, I wrapped the sandwich in aluminum foil to keep it warm and took it to the funeral home. Paul met me in the parking lot and I gave him the sandwich. He stood there, and without waiting until he went back inside, he opened up the aluminum foil and, as he pulled the foil away, he discovered some of the cheese had stuck to the aluminum.

Let me say that again: *Some of the cheese had stuck to the aluminum.*

That was it. That's ALL that happened. There was no plague, no famine. No sudden natural disaster had taken place, destroying the lives of thousands of people. The car hadn't suddenly burst into flames. Nope. What happened? *Some cheese from his sandwich had gotten stuck to the aluminum.*

Once again, what happened next was not only totally unjustifiable, it was also *grossly* disproportionate to what was going on. It was an effect for which there could be no reasonable explanation. And so, as had happened before, Paul just *lost his mind* - again. Instantly he was enraged, swearing and screaming and working himself into a frenzy. Within seconds he had gotten so worked up that he took the bottle of coke that I had also given him and smashed it on the concrete, shattering it into a million pieces. I quickly turned and jumped in the car to get out of his way and maybe avoid some of the effects of his uncontrollable rage. But I was unsuccessful. He grabbed the door before I could close it, flung it open, and reached into the car, grabbing my necklace and - essentially - pulled me out of the car by my throat - like a *dog on a leash.*

While jerking me around, he continued swearing and screaming and telling me how stupid I was to do something *so horrible* as to allow cheese from his sandwich to get stuck to aluminum. He ordered me to pick up all the glass from the bottle, while his rant continued. At first, I refused, but then as he started to hit a whole new gear in his rage, I decided that wisdom was the greater part of valor in that situation and I reluctantly "submitted" to his infantile power play and painstakingly picked up the shattered glass. As soon as it was done, I was angry, hurt and humiliated. I, again, jumped in the car and drove off, crying all the way home and completely at a loss to understand what had just happened. The next day, just as before, it was as if nothing had happened.

For Paul, but not for me.

Not long after that, Paul left his work at the funeral home - without an alternative job in place (that would have required wisdom and maturity). Once again, he was unemployed - this time for six months. If you had asked him during that time what was going on, he would have told you that he was actively looking for other work and that there was just "nothing" available. But the truth was his efforts were casual, at best, and on top of that, he was being extremely particular about what *sort* of job he would be willing to take. Never mind that our finances were once again very tight because of his poor decision-making. And so, while he was allegedly trying his "hardest" to find a job, he managed to spend a lot of time working on old cars with his buddies. I put up with all of this for a little while, but eventually, and in spite of his terrible temper, I'd had enough. I called him out, expressing my great frustration with him and his unwillingness to just take *any* job to try and help out. His response was to go into another fit of rage, this time ending it by punching his fist straight through the sheetrock in the hallway.

Yeah. That always helps.

As usual, he moved on and "recovered" quickly from the incident. No apologies were made. No admission that his actions were completely out of control. Nothing.

Eventually, Paul did land a job, one that he didn't love, but he felt it was a better fit and it was work he was willing to do. Even so, and after taking six months to find that job, he still - almost *immediately* - started talking about moving back to the Gulf Coast where he had grown up. To be fair, I have to say I was not opposed to this idea. I had grown to love the Coast when I attended college. Many of my sorority sisters were from the area and we had spent many fun weekends there together.

Although I continued to be frustrated over Paul's vocational restlessness, I told him that I would be willing to move again - but only if he found a job *before* we made the move. So, he started looking right away. Nevertheless, I was the one that once again found work much more quickly. It just happened that the firm I was currently working for in Jackson had decided to open a branch on the Mississippi Gulf Coast. I approached one of the partners and told him that I would like to be considered for the branch manager position for that new office. In spite of my relatively brief time with them in Jackson, I somehow convinced them that I could take on this new position. And so, they agreed to give me a shot. Not long after that, Paul was offered a job with a different company. On the surface at least, it seemed like Paul had kept his end of the bargain.

We moved in the spring of 1989. While my optimism had taken a bit of a beating, I still had hope that this would *finally* be the place where Paul could get settled into a job that would make him happy and, consequently, work out well for the rest of the family. That was not to be, however. Not long after we moved, he quit his first job and took another, and then another. The restlessness was unbelievable. After several failed attempts at finding the "right" job, he was again out of work for a number of months.

The more this took place, the more complacent and even despondent he became. He increasingly pulled back from the little bit that he was doing around the house. The lawn started looking more and more abandoned - and so those responsibilities ended up in my lap as well. I can say, without exaggeration, that I was quite literally doing it all while he became more and more self-indulgent.

In spite of those realities, I still managed to find some happiness. I had a beautiful baby boy whose smile lit up my world. I was progressing in my career and was focusing on building my network in the community. I joined the Biloxi Rotary Club and would later become their first female President. I joined the Chamber of Commerce and began to volunteer for events that would help the community. In the spring of 1990, to my great surprise, I was selected for the Chamber's first Leadership Gulf Coast class. I didn't know it at the time, but that experience would catapult my career to a whole new level, as it provided a great opportunity to network with various "movers and shakers" in our community. The people and friendships forged there became a mutually supportive network that benefitted all of our careers and went a long way toward cementing our financial futures.

More to the point, however, it was my fellow classmates in this Leadership Gulf Coast class that convinced me that I should make my dream a reality. I had shared with my class over the ten months that we were together in this program that my dream had always been to eventually have my own firm and determine my own destiny. They, along with other mentors that I met through my involvement in LGC, encouraged me to make the leap of faith. And so, I did. In August 1991, at the age of 30, I made the leap. It was scary and, yet, the best business decision I have ever made.

It was also a big topic of discussion in my marriage. Paul still had not found a job that he was happy with and kept asking me if he could join me in my new accounting practice. I kept saying no, and that I didn't believe it was a good idea. He tried to make me feel bad about it, but I stuck to my decision.

It didn't take me very long to begin building my client base. My work with the Chamber, the LGC class and the Rotary club had helped to build my reputation, and I quickly learned what most business people come to learn: People want to work with people they *know* and *trust*.

My biggest challenge that first year in my practice was that I became pregnant with my second child. Those of you reading this are probably wondering why I would want to have another child with this man at this point in our marriage, and with all that I knew about his issues. Something had happened to solidify this decision - and it had nothing to do with Paul.

My father is an only child. I believe that is why he wanted to have a lot of children of his own. Although he had a wonderful childhood, I knew that he missed having siblings. Knowing that, I began to think about my son. I didn't want him to grow up without a sibling. There is something to the saying that, in a relationship, "Joy can be shared, and sorrows divided." My father had no one to divide that sorrow with when his parents died. Of course, we were there for him, but only a sibling can truly understand the loss of a parent.

I had always *wanted* to have two children for that reason. In spite of the imperfections in my marriage, I still wanted another child for my son and, honestly, for me. My children truly were my happiness and it would be doubled if I had two.

I was thrilled that I was pregnant again, but it was hard propping up a new business while pregnant. The expected joy of a new baby to love helped me to *make* it work. My beautiful daughter was born in October of 1992. It was another blessing in my life and another happy place I could turn to for fulfillment.

...And I was going to need it.

<u>Four</u>

Not long after I became pregnant with my daughter, I finally gave in to Paul's relentless badgering regarding his coming to work with me. Even though I still had major hesitations about it, I reasoned that I could at least ensure that he had a job, and I could possibly provide a work environment that would cure him of his unwillingness to stick with anything vocationally. And on the financial side, it meant I could expand my practice, and yet recycle those funds back into the family. Even though I had questions and doubts, it *seemed* like it could be a win-win situation.

So, I agreed to take him on, but only after we had a long conversation where I explained to him that this was still *my* practice, and that it was *my* license on the line. I made it clear that he could not be a partner in the practice unless he passed the CPA exam (Certified Public Accountant) and that, until then, he would have to be my employee and understand that role. He assured me that he understood all of that and would be a model employee and, to be fair, he was - at first. But over time it became clear that he resented the fact that the clients saw me as the Owner and him as an employee. That growing resentment began to affect both his attitude and actions at work.

One day he sat me down and said he had a new idea about how "our" business should operate. He "explained" that people in our community thought/assumed, because he was "the man", he was also the Owner of the business. As a result, he thought we could increase our client base if we made a couple of changes and, in effect, aligned our practice with this alleged public perception. What was his idea? He suggested that *he* should be the "face" of the business by being the one that met with the clients to discuss their needs, go over their tax returns, etc. Meanwhile, I would be somewhere in the back office doing the *actual* work.

Now, quite honestly, I was angered by his suggestion, for a number of reasons. For one thing, what he was pitching as a "public perception" issue that we could embrace to leverage our business had very little to do with "the business" or *actual* public perceptions and *everything* to do with his *wounded ego*. It wasn't the "community" that was making assumptions about who should run "our" business - it was him - despite the fact that he had neither the experience nor expertise to do so.

At any rate, even though his "idea" was terrible, I had learned enough by then to know that sometimes you can make a point more effectively through circumstance than dialogue. And so, rather than arguing with him about it and setting off yet another round of verbal abuse, I went along with his "suggestion". As it turned out, I had a client coming in the very next day to pick up her return and informed Paul we could implement his ideas right away. He was, of course, thrilled at how easily I had been convinced to embrace his plan. Again, I hadn't actually agreed with *any* of his observations, nor with his "plan" for increasing our business. But I had learned a few things along the way and maybe - just maybe - the circumstances would get through to him in a way that my words never could.

The next day my client came in, and Paul met her and said that he was going to be going over her tax return with her. I could hear everything that was said because the office was small, and I kept my door open. It didn't take long for the client to ask Paul a question about one of her deductions. That's where, what had only started, began to immediately unravel. Why? Because Paul had never bothered to learn the tax code. He preferred to do the easier work and leave the more difficult matters to me. And so, the next thing I heard was a chair being pushed back, and the words, "Excuse me just a minute." He then came into my office and asked me the client's question. I gave him the answer but did not elaborate on the other related questions that might arise. Paul went back and gave the answer to my client. As I expected, the client asked a related question. Again, Paul did not know the answer and had to come and ask for help again. After the third time, Paul reluctantly told the client that she might just want to meet with me. That was the end of the new plan.

It was a small victory, and short-lived. But one of the truths it reinforced to me was the ability - as I've already suggested - of using circumstances to effectively "speak" in ways that my voice never could, and without generating the negative consequences that so often resulted from our toxic conversations. In short, I was getting smarter about handling my frequently dysfunctional life, which is such a pathetic reality. Sadly, my brief success on this particular occasion would come back to haunt me as I was made to pay, many times over, for this and other blows to his ego.

Not long after, we were at home one evening and, after putting my son to bed, I began working on an IRS tax notice for one of my clients. Part of that involved looking through the client's payroll tax returns, which Paul had prepared because that was one of the things that he routinely did for all of our clients. As I read through it, I discovered an error that Paul had made, and I called him over to show it to him. It wasn't a big deal at all and my whole purpose in pointing it out to him was, simply, so he could amend the return the next day at the office. It was not my intent to belittle him or anything like that. In the detail-driven world of accounting, it is impossible to avoid making mistakes. Everybody does, including me. I was simply letting him know what he needed to do the next day to correct it.

Once more, any semblance of maturity or self-control went right out the window, as he quickly became furious with me for daring to say that he had made an error. The fury became a tirade complete with all manner of swearing and arm- waving and demonstrating - and all of this was, of course, aimed at me. Then, as if that wasn't enough, he grabbed the client's file and pointlessly ripped it to shreds.

Not surprisingly, all of the screaming and swearing woke up our 4-year-old son who didn't know *what* was going on, except that he could hear his father ranting and raving like a lunatic. He was, of course, frightened by all the commotion and began calling out and crying, and just wanted someone to hold him and assure him that things were okay. So, I went into my son's bedroom and crawled in bed with him to try and settle him down. Paul immediately came into the room and told me to leave our son alone and come back to *our* bedroom. I told him that I would be there when I had calmed our son down. He said that if I didn't come now *he would start screaming again and scare him worse*! I was furious at Paul, but in the moment, felt like I had no choice, as another round of this craziness would only frighten my son even more.

Reluctantly, I pulled away from my son even though he was begging me not to go. I tried to assure him that everything was fine and quickly hugged and kissed him again and said goodnight. On the way to our bedroom Paul *shoved* me - eight months pregnant, mind you - but he shoved me, anyway, and caused me to fall. I was just able to catch myself but badly sprained my wrist doing so. Was there any apology or remorse or sympathy? Of course, there wasn't.

My wrist quickly began swelling, and I was in a great deal of pain for several days afterward. I never did get it checked out, but just endured it. However, as painful as that was, the part that was far more hurtful to me, and which angers me the most, is that Paul would create a ridiculous scene like this *for no reason* except his own error and subsequent immaturity. And then, as happened on this and many other occasions, his outbursts would often result in one or both of our children being upset and frightened by what was going on. When I went to clean up the mess that *he created* and address the fear that *he caused* - he didn't care enough about his son to let me help him. He never thought once about what it does to a *mother* when you upset her children, forcing her to ignore their cries and, essentially, abandoning them. I knew that they were not only frightened, but also confused as to why, in addition to their father acting like a crazy man, their mother wasn't there for them. He never thought about those things because none of them mattered as much as his damned ego.

Finding Some Happiness

By now I knew that my marriage was never going to get better. Paul was never going to change. Nevertheless, I decided to see my glass as half full - as much as I was able - and to find whatever joy and happiness I could in other areas of my life. The first opportunity for doing so presented itself almost immediately as my beautiful daughter was born in October of that year. I was, of course, *thrilled*. I had always wanted to have two children, a boy first and then a girl - and I was fortunate that it turned out just as I had hoped. Indeed, long before they came along, I had already settled on names for both of them.

And now they were *both* here, and I was so *glad*. To be sure, the pain of my marriage was still there, but in spite of it all, my children remained my dearest treasures and were a source of joy in the midst of many dark moments. So, I devoted myself to them, showering them with an affection that sprang not only from my love for them, but also from a desire to try and make up for, or cancel out, or at least *muffle*, the oppressive, brooding darkness that just seemed to suck all of the air out of the room, and was never very far away. Of course, balancing my commitments at home and at work was a real juggling act, but I was determined to make them both work. If my marriage had been different, and if my husband had pursued a steady career, it might have played out differently. I would have spent more time than I did at home. But that wasn't my reality. I, imperfectly, did the best that I could to make a less than ideal situation work. At the time, I couldn't see any other choice.

While my children were my greatest source of joy, there were other avenues that I pursued, and which also provided a measure of satisfaction and fulfillment that kept me from just being overwhelmed with the realities of my dysfunctional marriage. I became actively engaged in public service projects for my community by volunteering with the local Chamber of Commerce and taking positions in non-profit organizations.

As I look back on it now, it was a good thing - and more than just *good,* it was just plain *therapeutic* to involve myself in serving other people, or the community in general. I *needed* things in my life that said there was a world *outside* of my sad situation. And that world offered opportunities for validation and a sense of worth and purpose that I was denied within my marriage. Not that marriage is the only place to find those things, but it certainly can, and should be, one place where it exists. Sadly, not only was it not on offer, my circumstances were such that self-worth and validation were frequently under attack. At home I was stepped on, ignored, shoved aside, muzzled or put on a shelf until "needed". Outside my home, I was encouraged to believe that I actually had a voice and that I mattered and could make a difference.

Along with the positive benefit that came from engaging with various community organizations, there were also opportunities for recognition and other positions on local for-profit and not-for-profit boards. I was developing a reputation as a smart, successful business woman on the Gulf Coast. Although I was appreciative of the recognition, and the opportunities that it brought, I could not share any of this with my husband. His envy and jealousy made it impossible for him to applaud my success or to be genuinely supportive. As the opportunities and appointments came along, it was *not* a topic of conversation in our home. I learned to keep those sorts of things to myself. If the shoe had been on the other foot - and he had been recognized for his accomplishments - I have no doubt it would have been a centerpiece of conversation in the home. But this was about me, and that wasn't as important.

A series of events later served to further confirm the truth of that statement. The year was 1995 and I was asked to join the board of a financial institution. This was the first time I was being asked to join a board that would actually pay me for my services to help them set annual strategic goals and monitor progress against those goals. In contrast to his reactions to everything else to this point, on *this* occasion Paul was happy. Why? *Because money was involved.*

Five years later, in 2000, I was asked to join the Holding Company board. I was forty years old and was thrilled to be given this opportunity. But soon after I began to get pressure from Paul every month. He wanted me to try and use my position to gain *him* a position on the board. He would relentlessly interrogate me about this after every meeting. Had I talked with the President of the company about it?

What did he say? Etc. I began to dread coming home from the board meetings because Paul simply refused to understand or accept that the system didn't work the way he thought it did. But once again, the issue here was him and his ego, and as in this case, money. Those were the things that mattered. My success and I were not important. *Worse*, they were an insult.

Despite these realities and the continuing lack of acknowledgment at home, in the business community I continued to gain momentum. My five-figure income became six and we were able, for the first time, to start putting away money for future plans and dreams. And yet, even as I share that detail, I think it is important to say in the same breath that money **absolutely** does not make you happier - a lesson I learned the hard way. Once my business took off, I never looked back financially.

But let me tell you: it wasn't a source of happiness for me. In fact, in many ways it was the opposite and was often a source of grief and discord. Here I was, working hard as the primary source of our financial success, and yet, I benefitted the least from my labors. Paul would go out and buy whatever he wanted - boats, cars, jet skis - whatever. But if I wanted a new lamp for the house, I had to make a case for it. I literally had to ask permission to spend the money I had made! *Everything* was a negotiation with him. I had to get him to sign off on anything I wanted to buy for myself, the kids, or the house.

This was, understandably, a huge source of frustration for me.

With every extravagant purchase he made, and every basic purchase I had to fight tooth and nail for, it became increasingly clear that Paul valued the *money* more than he valued the one who made it. His wants were assumed and non-negotiable. Everything else - including things for the children - well, "We're just going to have to think about that..."

Another way money, or at least Paul's handling of it, became a source of discord was seen in the way it became the currency by which he demonstrated a clear favoritism for his son over his daughter. I started noticing how Paul would spend a lot more money on our son for his presents or his wants than he was *ever* willing to do for our daughter. And the sad part is that our daughter saw it too. *Clearly.*

For example, we would be on a vacation in Florida (something we did regularly because that is what Paul liked to do) - but we would go on these vacations and eventually find ourselves in a souvenir shop at some point. Paul would purchase *whatever* our son wanted, but would only allow me to buy inexpensive, small things for our daughter. He would tell her that she really didn't need the more expensive item she wanted. There was a clear double standard, and it was painful to realize that Paul simply did not value our daughter as much as our son. Why? Because she was a FEMALE. So, to combat that, I began to buy her things behind his back. I told her not to tell her father, and *she understood why*. That always broke my heart: that she was shown at such a young age that her father did not see her as her brother's equal.

Stepping back to take in a bigger perspective, it was sad - not only because of the hurt that it inflicted on my daughter, which was bad enough - but because his favoritism created an unhealthy family dynamic that put me in a situation where I had to "hide" things from my husband. And worse, I had to form a secret alliance with my daughter to keep certain things from her father. No parent should feel like they have to do that sort of thing for their children, and no child should have to be in a situation where they are asked to "choose" or engage in activities that are so psychologically perilous.

All of which is to say: the financial success I was having, while helpful in many ways, was also a catalyst for further dysfunctionality in an already bad situation. It didn't *have* to be that way. But in our home, it was.

Escalation of the Abuse

While all of these things were going on, within the home the *verbal* abuse continued to escalate, and frighteningly, so did the instances of physical abuse. I had been punched in the arm in the midst of yet another pointless tirade. At other times he would grab me by the shoulder or arm and squeeze as hard as he could, until I cried out in pain. And sometimes, as he was breaking some object or shattering some glass in a fit of explosive anger, I would be cut by the flying shrapnel. As I said before, it didn't happen every day or every week, but it shouldn't have happened at all. It happened with enough frequency to keep me constantly on edge. Imagine living in a house where you knew, at any moment, a battle could break out. And you don't know where or when. That's what it was like. Explosive anger. Destructive anger. And I could rarely see it coming.

Neither could my children. One consequence of this unhealthy environment was that they began to stay in their rooms at night. They weren't safe there, but I think they felt *safer*. They rarely came out to sit with us or watch television. Now, to be sure, some of that was a function of age and just kids being kids. My son, for example, was now thirteen years old and he, like many children that age, preferred staying in his room. As I later reflected on this, it became quite obvious to me that this behavior was more about providing a safe haven for my daughter and a judgement-free zone for my son.

But the bigger factor in all of that, I know, was the anger, tension and the extremely volatile atmosphere in our home that was *always* there. It felt like we were imprisoned between the four walls of our house in a "cage" of violence that would erupt without any warning and we were left with no escape plan. You just never knew when something would send "Dad" into an insane rage. So, it was just safer to stay out of the way and try not to screw up.

As for my daughter, she was terrified of her father and preferred to spend time with her brother in his room because she clearly felt safer there. I did not, at that time, have any idea *how* afraid she was. That wouldn't become evident until later on. I don't know why, but I naively thought that, because our fights were often taking place behind closed doors, that this provided some sort of insulation for the kids. But as the fights escalated, and as I began to fight back, they became louder, and longer, and cuss words were flying left and right. They heard every word of it - they heard the sounds of things smashing against walls, and, occasionally, his fist going through sheetrock. The door may have been closed for many of those fights, but you cannot contain the consequences of anger and violence simply by closing a door. You can't.

There were other things that happened during this period that produced defining moments for me. One of them happened in the midst of one of our frequent fights. Up to this point I had become accustomed, sadly, to the fact that Paul would punch holes in walls, or break things, or throw them when he was acting out his rage. I'm not saying I ever got "used" to it. I'm just saying that it wasn't surprising to me that it kept taking place.

But on one particular occasion, things had gotten really bad, and I could see in Paul's eyes that he really, truly, *hated* me and was just barely restraining himself from hitting me. What he did next was almost as bad and, in some ways, worse than hitting me. Paul looked at the paintings above our bed. I knew what he was thinking. My mother, who was/is a very talented artist, had lovingly created and given these to me, to treasure and keep. Paul knew how much they meant to me. He reached up and took one off the wall. I began begging him not to do anything to the painting. Paul just looked at me *and began smashing the frame to pieces against the wooden footboard of the bed and shredded it, right in front of me.* I was devastated. This was yet another step in the evolution of his anger. This wasn't just anger. This was spite. This was vindictive, hateful, *vicious.* This felt like an attack, not only on me, but my mother and indeed my whole family. To take something like that – something that cannot be replaced and has such meaning to a person, and just callously destroy it - that crosses a line, a different line. It was *cruelty* of the worst sort. The kind that changes your perspective by the heartless nature of it.

That hurt me, deeply, and in a new way. And it changed me. It left a deep scar *inside of me.* One that I would never forget and one that I did not think could ever be healed. I looked at him differently from that day forward.

The other thing that happened was that I turned 40. As is the case for many people, when you reach a milestone in growing older, it is often an occasion for reflection and decision and *change.* It certainly was for me. But it didn't happen over a long period of time. It was more like a switch got thrown. When I turned 40, something inside me snapped. Something inside me started to *whisper* that enough was enough. That whisper would one day grow into a roar. In short, I decided to not be afraid anymore, or at least to not show it, and to no longer put up with the nonsense.

I was no longer willing to put up with someone telling me I was stupid, monitoring my every move and telling me what to do twenty-four hours a day. I was no longer willing to just "manage" a horrible situation. I was over it. Things would have to get better, or else.

Not surprisingly, my newfound perspective had an effect on Paul. And, it wasn't a good one. The fact that I wasn't going to show him fear anymore upset him and threw him off. I think he genuinely started to experience some fear himself - fear that he was losing control of a situation that he thought he had locked down. And *that* fear caused him to become even more extreme in his demonstrations of anger and violence. In spite of all that, my mind was made up. As I said, things were going to have to get better, or else.

Unfortunately, as I came to see, sometimes things have to get worse before they get better.

Five

It seems like every generation has at least one defining moment. Out of the blue, something completely unexpected happens, blindsiding the entire planet. From that day forward, nothing is ever the same.

The world is suddenly, and permanently, *different*.

For my grandparents, that day was December 7th, 1941 - the attack on Pearl Harbor. For my parents, it was November 22nd, 1963 - the day Kennedy was shot. For anyone reading this page, September 11th, 2001 was the defining moment. It certainly was for me. To be sure, I was actually alive when Kennedy was shot, but I was too young for it to have an impact. As far as I was concerned, my world was still a safe place.

Then 9/11 came along and, to borrow a line from a song by Don Henley and Bruce Hornsby, it was "the end of the innocence". Things that I had watched and heard about happening in *other* countries all my life had now taken place in our *own* backyard. So, for days we were all glued to our TV's, watching the horrific scenes, grieving the terrible loss of life, reeling from the hatred that had perpetrated it and wondering what it all meant. In time the initial shock faded, and we all - somehow - figured out a way to move forward with our lives and, cautiously and tentatively, *we did*.

But the world *had* changed, and things had been set in motion that would impact all of us, on large and small scales, internationally and interpersonally.

The following spring, I was on what had become an annual ski trip with my girlfriends. As usual, it was a great trip, and we all enjoyed the change of pace. And yet, even in *that* context, I remember hearing and watching daily reports about the most recent developments in the Middle East, especially with regard to our country's ongoing involvement there. Little did I know that the involvement was about to become more personal than ever.

Upon returning home from that trip, Paul, who had also been keeping up with developments in the Middle East for some time, suddenly announced that he wanted to serve his country once again and join in the efforts. To fill in the blanks for you here: When Paul left the Naval Aviation program years before he still kept his hand "in the game", so to speak, by joining the Navy Reserves. The possibility of this sort of thing was always there in the background.

Nevertheless, his sudden announcement still came as a huge surprise to me. I simply hadn't seen it coming and, to this day, I am not sure why he *really* wanted to do this. Maybe the events of 9/11 had been percolating inside him for some time and he felt a sense of patriotic duty. Or maybe it wasn't anything as noble as that. Perhaps he just wanted a change of pace. That would certainly have been consistent with his pattern up to that point. The truth is, I didn't know at the time, and I still don't know *why*.

But what I *did* know was that once the initial shock of his announcement wore off, I started thinking about it. And the more I thought about it, the more I felt an undeniable sense of *relief* wash over me as I contemplated the possibility that he might be gone - away from the house, away from us - for a significant amount of time.

Perhaps it sounds terrible to admit that, but honestly, given what had transpired thus far in our marriage, that is how the news affected me. I began to think about how different it would be, or at least *could* be. I felt a sense of hope that there might finally be some *peace* in our home. I thought about what it might be like to NOT have to walk around on eggshells all the time, wondering when the next explosive, childish outburst would take place.

Even as I write these things, I am conscious of the fact that for many and perhaps most people who have sent loved ones to participate in the military efforts overseas, their experiences were likely very different than my own. And I do not wish to minimize *at all* the huge sacrifices that have been made by so many in that regard, including the ultimate sacrifice. It isn't that I wanted *harm* to come to Paul, nor that I wouldn't have been *grieved* if it had.

But the reality is that our home had become a battlefield of its own. There were skirmishes on an almost daily basis, and often over the most trivial of things. Someone moved the pen (heaven forbid) that was *supposed* to remain by the phone so that notes could be taken down when needed. That was my fault, apparently, and led to a *ridiculously* disproportional fight. The motor on his big, red cigarette boat was not working right. That was, somehow, my fault too. Seemingly, everything was my fault; even when it wasn't. There was always something wrong, and the fighting that ensued continued to grow and grow in frequency, intensity and *pettiness*.

And so, in *that* context, the possibility of his going overseas was not unhappy news for me. Indeed, as I look back on it now, the irony does not escape me that Paul's active re-engagement with the military overseas translated into a reprieve from the hostilities *in my own home*.

So, within a very short amount of time, the decision was made, and Paul left for Qatar. While having a whole year of relative peace to think about my life and future was a welcome change, I also knew that it would not be easy. I was already doing the lion's share of things at *home*, but now I would also have to keep a business built for two up and running all by myself. But somehow, I managed.

Paul was gone for quite a while. And yet, while Paul was no longer physically present, his *presence* was still felt. He would call me, at least once a week, from halfway around the world to make sure that I was doing all of the things that I needed to do, according to him. He was very concerned that I was not spending money needlessly on someone to help with the house, yard, children or business. Those calls were exhausting, and I dreaded them each week. We did see Paul several times that year, but it was always around some fun event and never so that he could just come home to "help out". Not once when he came back did he pitch in and help. I still don't think he ever realized how frustrating that was *for* me, or how revealing that was *to* me.

However, in spite of all of the things I had to do, and how tired I was on a daily basis, and the weekly interrogations, I still enjoyed the peacefulness of our household. Indeed, one of the clearest indicators of how Paul's absence had changed the dynamic of our home was the simple fact that the children's behavior changed dramatically. Instead of retreating to their rooms as they typically did when Paul came home in the evening, they started coming out of their rooms at night. The family room *became* a family room for the first time. We watched television, laughed and interacted in ways that we had not done before. Honestly, it was a wonderful year.

To be sure, it wasn't as if Paul was completely ignored or forgotten. That was hardly possible. Things were just better.... far better. And, even though our marriage was terribly difficult and hugely disappointing, I hadn't completely given up on it *yet*, even though I had serious and growing misgivings. This was evidenced by the fact that it was *during* this time that things were so much better that I still had a desire to take up a project just for him. I decided to cross-stitch a Navy Crest as a present for him when he returned home. The back story there was that I had made one for my Dad, years before, when he retired from the Navy Reserve as a Captain. And Paul had always been envious that I had done that for my father but had never made one for him.

And so, while Paul was gone, I would sit down late at night, after getting the kids to bed, and I would work on the crest. Paul came back home right before Christmas and, even though I had not quite finished the crest, I wrapped it in a box and put it under the Christmas tree anyway. He seemed pleasantly surprised on Christmas morning when he opened it, and I assured him that I would finish it quickly and get it framed. For the moment, it seemed I had done something right. But that moment was fleeting.

Now that Paul's tour of duty was over, things quickly reverted "back to *normal*" at home. It didn't take long for the former oppressive atmosphere to return. But things didn't just return to where they were before. *If only*. The reality is that they were now much worse - for three main reasons. First, Paul was moodier than he had ever been and his restlessness, which had always been pretty prevalent, was more pronounced, as was his irritability.

But there was another change that was even more disturbing to me: his *perspective*. Based on his very limited exposure to another culture during his time away, Paul had formed some new and pretty extreme conclusions on a number of matters. For example, he announced one day that women in the Middle East were blissfully happy with their lifestyle. He talked about how they were well cared-for, loved, and respected, and that they did not mind the fact that men completely controlled their lives. Of course, he had no way of actually knowing these things, but that didn't stop him from asserting them - with great certainty.

Further, he said that they were happy to be told what to do, where they could go, and when to speak. He then tried to convince me that I needed to begin "acting the way women in the Middle East did with their husbands" - at least as he saw it. He asserted that I needed to defer to my husband's every wish, whether I agreed with it or not.

As you can imagine, this new *perspective* did not sit very well with me, to put it mildly. As a result, we had many arguments about this and the more I resisted his efforts to make me see things his way, the angrier he became. I knew *why* he was angry, of course. His newfound perspective, if only I would adopt it, would have created the perfect existence for him. He would have a wife that obeyed his every command, without question and without argument. If I would just cooperate....

That wasn't going to happen. You see, Paul wasn't the only one who had experienced a change in perspective. The previous year had given me a taste of what life *could* be like and, consequently, a deeper insight into how terribly *dysfunctional* our marriage had been. I knew it was bad, of course, but having a reprieve for a full year only seemed to highlight the troubled nature of our existence all the more. Now that I knew what was *possible* and what had been *missing*, I wasn't about to just roll over and play dead. I was finally ready to start fighting back.

This was the third reason that things were worse than before. While I was still fearful, at times, of his anger and what he might be capable of, during his absence I had become more fearful of something else: who I had become, what I was becoming, and what was happening to my children by *not* fighting back - for me and for them. I realized that "keeping the peace" was a failed strategy and had accomplished nothing.

Another big event during Paul's time away was that our son turned sixteen and got his driver's license. With Paul still overseas, it made sense for our son to just use his father's car for the time being. So, he did. But now that Paul was back home, we were one car short. Consequently, I told Paul, and he agreed, that he needed to find a vehicle for our son as soon as he was able. Given Paul's love for cars, I thought that should have been an *easy* and *enjoyable* thing for him to do.

As it turned out, it wasn't. I kept waiting and asking and reminding him - and Paul simply refused to get the job done. I couldn't understand what the reluctance was. It certainly wasn't about the money. We could easily afford it. He kept telling me things that just didn't make sense. For example, he said that he didn't know what he wanted, or which one to get. And I thought, "The car isn't for YOU, it's for our son. Ask *him* what he wants, and I bet he can tell you in a moment." Still, he drug his feet. In frustration, finally, I told him we could just rent a vehicle until he could make up his mind. Even this didn't produce an answer to the transportation issue. I don't know if he was doing it to be difficult or if he was trying to make some point. But, whatever the reason, the job didn't get done. This meant that our son had to start catching rides to and from high school again.

A couple of months later, while our son was riding home in the back of his best friend's sister's car, they got into an accident. The vehicle rolled, and our son ended up in the hospital with a broken collarbone. Paul felt horrible about this. He knew that I was irritated with him because he had not bought or rented a car that would have allowed our son to drive himself. I didn't tell him that, but I didn't have to. He knew he was the reason that our son was in someone else's car.

I tell you this story because it was probably the closest Paul ever came to admitting he was wrong about anything. And I honestly think one of the reasons he was so upset about the whole incident is because it exposed him a little bit and backed him into a corner - and he didn't like that at all, as I would soon find out.

A few weeks later, I was finishing up the Navy crest cross-stitch while I watched TV one night. Out of the blue Paul proceeded to tell me that he had filed a lawsuit against our son's best friend's parents regarding the accident. I asked him what he was talking about. He said that he was going to get our son's college money from that family. I then reminded him that our son's college money was in the bank already. I asked him if he put my name on the lawsuit. He said "Yes". I then told him that I would not be party to a frivolous lawsuit - these were friends of ours, and our son's best friend's family. I said that he needed to call the attorney the next day and take my name off of the lawsuit. He refused. I then told him that I would testify *against him* if he did not.

That's when it got ugly. He began by throwing the TV remote at the TV screen, smashing it. He then got up and snatched the cross-stitch out of my hands, went into the kitchen and began to rip it up with a butcher's knife. I was screaming at him, begging him to please stop. He didn't. Then he pushed me up against the counter, screaming at me, and held the knife at my throat.

Out of the corner of my eye, I saw my children come out of my son's bedroom with fear on their faces. My son headed to our bedroom. *I knew he was going to get the gun.* I had to defuse the situation. As much as it degraded me to do so, I gave in; I told Paul that he was right, and I was wrong. I told my son that it would all be okay. I admitted, in front of my children, that this was all my fault.....even though I knew it wasn't. At that point, I would have done anything to save my children from what could have been a terrible outcome.

But I was seething inside. Who was this monster I had married?

The next day I carried on like nothing had happened. As always, I kept the peace and wore a happy face on the outside. *Inside was a different story.* I was filled with turmoil. My mind was racing. I didn't know what to do, but I knew this lifestyle was no longer acceptable. The events of the previous night had left their mark. A line was crossed. For me, it was a point of no return. I wasn't sure what I was going to do just yet, but I knew I had to do *something*.

The following week another event occurred, that underscored the conclusion I had already reached. My Dad, who was a Dentist, called my cell phone and asked to speak to Paul. As a precursor to this event, I should tell you that my Dad is a kind and wonderful man. He doesn't have a mean bone in his body. He does love a good joke, but he never has any ill will. I gave the phone to Paul and quickly realized, from my side of the conversation, that something was going very wrong.

My father had told Paul about a new patient that had told him a story from when Paul and his siblings were in high school. My father thought the story was funny and was ribbing Paul about it. The man said that he was renting a house next door to Paul's family home, which was owned by Paul's parents. Paul's mother had found some marijuana plants in their flowerbed and had said something about it to their tenant. When Paul heard that this patient had shared this particular story with my father - for some reason - he went ballistic. He started yelling and cussing at my father. He demanded that my father tell him the name of the tenant so he could "Kick his Ass!". Of course, my father refused. When he did so, Paul told him that he would never see his grandchildren again until he gave Paul the man's name. I grabbed the phone from Paul, apologized to my Dad, and told him everything would be okay. I called my father back as soon as I was alone to apologize.

I was livid but did not discuss it while Paul was in such an agitated state. I got everyone to bed and hoped and prayed that things would calm down the next day while I tried to figure out what to do. Things did calm down - a little - but only because I was working overtime to manage the craziness. My efforts, sadly, were short-lived.

The very next week Paul and I went to a dear friend's 40th birthday party. On the drive home Paul announced to me that he had decided to take the kids to Gulf Shores the following weekend. I told him that they couldn't go that weekend because they would be at my parent's house for the annual "Grandkids Sleepover". Paul informed me that they were not going this year, or ever again, unless my Dad gave him the name of the patient. I became very angry. I told Paul that MY kids would see MY parents anytime I wanted them to or they wanted to. He didn't expect that out of me. He immediately started yelling and cussing and telling me that I would do whatever **HE** wanted. (You get the picture.)

Inevitably, the fight escalated, and became toxic *very* quickly because, for the first time, I held my ground, and kept holding it, refusing to back down. I was not going to let him bully me into taking my kids away from their grandparents. He was being completely ridiculous. And I was sick and tired of being told what I would or would not do by a man for whom I no longer had any respect. So, the more he screamed, the more I screamed right back. I told him that he was crazy - that he had lost his mind. At that, he clenched his fist and smashed it into the windshield, as he was driving. *Instantly it shattered.* We were just pulling up to a stoplight, he slammed on the brakes, leaned over and slugged me in my arm. I sat there, stunned at all that had just happened, my arm throbbing with pain. I didn't know what to do. Suddenly the light turned green and Paul let off the brake, but before he could get going forward, in desperation, I threw the car door open and jumped out. He rolled the window down and started screaming at me to get back in the car. When I refused, he drove home. I walked the rest of the way. When I got there, I didn't speak a word and spent the rest of the afternoon avoiding and ignoring him.

That evening I slept on the couch. I wasn't about to share a bed with this man I no longer knew. I slept very little that night. Too many things were going through my mind. The next morning was Saturday. It was Paul's Navy Reserve drill weekend, which meant he would be gone all day Saturday and Sunday. I was still trying to process all that had happened. On the one hand I felt paralyzed and, at the same time, I felt panicked - like I wanted to run, but couldn't. I spent the entire morning crying on the porch. I had to make a big decision and I had to make it NOW. I now saw that things were never going to change. I had asked Paul to go to couple's therapy many times in the past and he had always refused. So that was never going to be an option. And all of my foolish thoughts that I might be able to change him had proven to be woefully naive. I had spent, at least, the past ten years praying, almost daily, for some sort of divine intervention - either by God changing Paul or somehow changing me - anything to bring some sort of relief. But nothing had happened. Nothing was working, and things were now far worse than they had ever been. There was no way Paul was going to change. And there was no way I was going to put up with it any longer.

I had made my decision. I had to leave, or he had to leave, but we could not stay together, and my children could not remain in this situation. There was no time to lose. I dried my tears, put a smile on my face, fixed the kids breakfast, and told my son that his sister and I had some errands to run. My daughter was only eleven years old at the time and was quite fragile, having been emotionally terrorized by her father - certainly more so than her brother. Because of that, I felt the need to keep her near me, especially now, and if I did that, I also knew I would have to impress upon her the importance of keeping my plans a secret.

So, she accompanied me all that day. The first thing I did was separate the cash in our accounts, splitting it 50/50. To facilitate that, I opened up new accounts in my name only and transferred my half into them at our two banks. Even though I had earned most of it, this wasn't about the money. This was about "getting out", and it was going to be hard enough to pull this off without adding a distracting battle over who gets what.

I then drove around town looking at apartment complexes. I needed to find an apartment that was safe and large enough that the kids would have their own bedrooms. As it turns out, I couldn't find an apartment that offered enough security; I was so afraid that he would come after me. I had to find a place where we could be safe. I ended up calling my sister, who lived about 30 minutes away, and asked if we could come stay with her and her family. She said, "Of course.", and wondered why I hadn't called her first. I explained that I didn't want them to be in any danger because of my situation. She replied that we would deal with whatever happened, and that I needed to be with family. I have never forgotten that day - the day my sister and her husband became the safe haven for my children, Tasha (our dog) and me.

We had been gone all day and wouldn't be home before nightfall. Paul would be back soon, and I wouldn't have time to leave before he got home. I couldn't leave my son with him; I didn't trust what he might do and would never put my children at risk. On the way home I told my daughter, again, that she would have to keep a big secret. I explained to her that her father could never know what we had been doing that day and she assured me that she could keep our secret. I asked if she was upset and she told me she wasn't. She said she just wanted me "to be happy". Looking back, her *willingness* to be my accomplice, against her own father, was a revelation of just how terrible things had become.

Paul arrived home shortly after and, even though I had prepped my daughter for this situation, I was still terrified that she might slip-up and tell him what we had done that day. After all, she was only a child. But she didn't. She could have won an Oscar for her performance that night. What a smart and brave girl! Even at her young age, she knew that the situation between her Mom and Dad was just about as wrong as it could be.

The time passed slowly as I watched the clock - trying to look calm and normal on the outside and yet feeling nothing but turmoil inside. Finally, the kids went to sleep, and Paul asked if I was coming to bed. I said "No" and informed him that I would be sleeping on the couch. I was civil, but there was no warmth in my voice. He could feel the chill and, frankly, I was glad he felt it. I'm sure he must have *suspected* that *something* was going on with me, because I had never slept on the couch two nights in a row. He was agitated, but elected not to say anything, and disappeared into the bedroom. After he left the room I felt the *slightest* sense of accomplishment and, honestly, felt more like *myself* in that small moment than I had in quite a while.

I could have gone to my sister's the next day, but I felt like I needed another day of reflection. It was a huge decision I was making - with permanent ramifications - and I think I was seeking some sort of validation from my family and friends that I hadn't lost my mind. I called my dear friend, Patti, my brother and both of my sisters. I also called my parents. I wanted to know what the people closest to me thought so I asked for their advice. At the end of the day, I got the verification I was hoping for and began to feel a sense of relief that I was doing the "right" thing.

That night Paul came home again from his drill and everything occurred similarly to the previous night. At the end of the evening he got up to go to bed and, again, asked if I would be joining him. Once more, I said "No." I asked if he had come to his senses about his proclamation that my children would never see their grandparents again. He said that he had not and shut the bedroom door.

I didn't sleep a single minute that night. Instead, I lay in the dark thinking about what had to happen next. What was the safest way to leave? Would he come after me? How would I defuse his anger? Lots of questions went through my mind, but I somehow managed to corral my thoughts enough to formulate an exit strategy. I got up off the couch around 2 A.M. and wrote Paul a note. I then carefully hid that note where Paul would not find it *until I wanted him to*. I went back to the couch and stared into the darkness until the sun came up.

Even though I was physically exhausted, with the sunshine came a renewed sense of energy and *conviction*. I knew I was going down a path from which there would be no return. Once I left, there was no way I was coming back, both because I knew this was the right decision and, more pragmatically, because I knew in my gut that if I did, there would be a new kind of hell to pay, and any future attempt to escape would probably cost me my life.

Paul woke up and got dressed for work. It was summer; the kids were still sleeping so it was just the two of us. He was surprised to discover me in the kitchen, drinking coffee, but not making any efforts to get ready for work. He commented on it and asked if I was going to the office. I told him I was not. I said that I needed a day off. If he didn't know that something was really wrong before, he did now, or he should have. I *never* stayed home from work unless I was deathly ill. Never.

If he was concerned, he didn't show it and, after getting some things together, he got ready to leave. Just moments before I had uttered a simple, silent prayer. I had asked God to please give me a sign that I was doing the right thing. As Paul started to walk out the door I said, "I will ask you one more time: Will you go to couple's therapy with me?" He said, "No, there is nothing wrong with me. I am *perfect*. You, however, may need therapy."

I silently thanked God for my answer.

<u>Six</u>

I waited until I heard his car pulling out of the driveway, peeked out the window, and then got to work. I dressed quickly, feeling both nervousness and something *else* I couldn't quite put my finger on. "Excitement" wouldn't be the right word, but there was a faint hopefulness about stepping into a strange and unknown future. I had no idea how any of this would play out, but I was at that place where "anywhere but here" and "anything but this" seemed like the far better option.

After dressing, I quickly retrieved the note I had written and placed it on the kitchen counter. In it I said that the children and I were leaving to go and stay with my sister for a few days. I explained that I wanted a six-month separation so that I could have time to think about what I wanted in my future and for my children's future. Privately, I knew that I would never go back, but I wanted to let Paul have time to process the changes that were coming and hoped that telling him I just wanted to separate for a while might not set him off quite as much as my telling him it was completely *over*. His temper was truly frightening, and I was just trying to do whatever I could to keep my children and myself out of its path.

As an additional precaution, I had called the Chief of Police and the Sheriff the day before

I left. I knew them both very well and briefly explained what was about to occur and why. I also gave them my sister's address and asked them to please take very seriously any call that came from my phone, especially over the next 2 to3 days. They assured me that they would be vigilant if they received any call from me, which made me feel better, but didn't totally alleviate my fears.

And just to be clear: I didn't make those calls in an attempt to ruin Paul or his reputation. He could handle that all by himself. It was simply that I had witnessed his craziness too many times before and recalled very vividly the day that he told me he would kill me if I ever left him. I had no reason to doubt that he might actually do it. And when he discovered I had taken half of the money from our accounts - I knew that would probably put him over the edge, even more than the thought of losing me or the kids. That's a sad admission to make. But I really did feel that it was true and, unfortunately, the passage of time has confirmed that hypothesis.

All of that - and more - was running through my mind as I hurried to wake the kids and tell them what was happening. My son, because he was hearing about all of this for the first time was, understandably, very upset with me. He knew there had been issues - serious issues - between his father and me for a long time. He had witnessed, and been on the receiving end of, his father's anger on any number of occasions. Nevertheless, he still didn't want his parents to go through a divorce. He had seen that happen enough to his friends and had some idea what that might look like and didn't want any part of it. But I held my ground and told him he was going with me and that there wasn't going to be any discussion on that point. He would understand *in time*.

My daughter, the dog and I got in my car and headed to my sister's house. My son got in his car and dutifully followed. He was not happy about it, but he did obey me. Looking back on that, I realize now how fragile my escape plans really were on that particular point. I hadn't really thought through what I would have done if he had dug his heels in and refused to go. The only thing I know for sure is that I would have never left him there, and I'm grateful he didn't challenge me that day. There's simply no telling how differently things might have worked out if he had.

Once we got on the road, I started crying. My daughter, who was eleven at the time, asked me what was wrong. I told her that I just didn't know if I was "doing the right thing." Without missing a beat, she responded with the kind of surprising insight that children sometimes come up with. She very matter-of-factly said "Look, Mom, now my brother will not grow up to *be* like Dad, and I won't end up *marrying* someone like Dad. And, you will be happy. What's wrong with that?"

Indeed. What *was* wrong with that? Instantly, my tears dried up. I couldn't decide if my daughter was just a very clever young girl, or if God was sending me a message. I now think it was both.

Sizing up the situation

The note I had left for Paul asked him to give me a few days to reflect on my options and what I wanted in my future. Of course, Paul did not honor that request. Once he arrived home that afternoon and saw the note, the phone calls began. He called me repeatedly, but I refused to answer. He then began calling our son, and after that my sister, and then her husband. When I still refused to talk he began calling our friends, my girlfriends and other family members, pressuring them all to call me.

It was exhausting. I was emotional and scared, and I just wanted a few days to get my head cleared and figure out what to do next. Paul was determined to not let that happen. His badgering and pursuit of me those first few days was brutal. And when night came, it offered little relief, as sleep proved to be quite elusive.

It was during this period that my brother-in-law suggested that I begin writing a journal everyday of what had *been* going on and what *was* happening now. He felt that it might help me to get my thoughts together as well as provide some sort of outlet for the intense and varied emotions I was experiencing. As it turned out, that was a great suggestion, and it actually *did* help to calm me down, at least a little. It was a relief to be in an environment that was safe, nonjudgmental, free from questions - and interrogations - and just plain *quiet.*

Somewhere in the midst of that calm I managed to put together an email telling Paul of my frustrations with him and how I did not appreciate his relentless badgering and recruiting/pressuring other people to carry out his agenda. I didn't need that, not that he cared. I also told him I wasn't going to respond and if he wanted to communicate with me he would have to settle for doing so by email.

On the fourth night at my sister's house I was invited to a party that was being hosted by a good friend of hers. The whole family had been invited and they convinced me to go with them, thinking it might be a good diversion for the kids and me to do something that felt kind of normal. I needed a change of pace, a respite from the constant questions and worries rolling around in my brain, so we accompanied them to the party.

Unfortunately, what could have been a nice reprieve for those few hours never materialized. Not long after we arrived I got a phone call from Paul's father, with whom I had always maintained a decent relationship, so I took the call. At first, he was kind, and the call was civil, up to the point where he realized that I was not to be swayed. Then his tone began to change – it became cold and almost matter-of-fact. He told me that I needed to understand that he would have to side with his son and that one of the implications, if I went on to divorce Paul, was that he and I would probably never speak again. I told him that I understood. He then asked if I would be willing to at least talk to Paul one time on the phone and, reluctantly, I agreed.

In the next instant, Paul was on the phone. He had, apparently, been sitting there with his father the whole time. I was mad. I didn't like being set up like that, but I stayed on the line for what was a brief *conversation* - if you could call it that. What it *really* amounted to was a monologue where Paul made it crystal clear that he was not at all concerned about me, or the reasons that I left. *If* I wasn't going to be his do-as-you're-told wife, house manager, cook, cleaner, maid, nanny and concubine; he didn't want me. The one thing he *was* concerned about was money and how all this would affect him financially. He had it *really* good - because of me - and he didn't want to lose what the money provided. So, he tried, vainly, to guilt me into coming back by saying that I would be the first in his family to "ever get a divorce". But I was unmoved and, when he realized he wasn't getting anywhere, he hung up.

For the next couple of weeks, and before school started up again, I tried to put on a happy face for the kids and did whatever I could to involve them in activities I knew they would enjoy. It was challenging at times, because we had to fit things in around my son's summer

104

work schedule, but we made the most of it. I had contacted my clients to let them know why I would not be in the office for a couple of weeks and had given them my cell phone number. They were all very gracious and supportive of my need to take care of my family situation first.

It was somewhere during that time-period that my son surprised me with a sweet card containing a gift certificate. He was working at a local resort and had very generously and thoughtfully sacrificed some of his hard-earned money to get me a massage treatment at their spa. Even in the midst of his own hurt and mixed emotions, he knew how hard all of this was for me and wanted to do something sweet. Of course, I broke into tears, but this time they were happy and thankful tears. I will never forget that moment and feeling so grateful - not just for his gift – but, more importantly, for him doing something that gave me hope that somewhere, on the other side of whatever the next months and years might bring, there would be a place where there was acceptance, understanding and peace.

One of the largest undertakings during that period was choosing an attorney and setting an appointment to sit down to discuss my options. When we met I told him that I wanted a separation - at least for a while - and *then* I would file for divorce. I was certain that a separation would not fix our problems, but I wanted to stick to my word because that sort of thing has always mattered to me.

However, in spite of my best intentions, it simply was not to be. As I discovered, in the state of Mississippi there is no provision for separation. You're either married or divorced. So, my attorney informed me that I would *have* to file for a divorce, but could back out of it later, if I wanted. If I wanted to get Paul to leave the house and give me the time I needed to figure out everything, I would have to file for a divorce, unless he would willingly move out - which he had already refused to do.

So, I did what I had to. The kids needed to be back in their home. With their whole world being overturned, they needed *something* that *wasn't* changing, something solid. I had told Paul he could take any or all of the furniture he wanted in the house with him, just not the kids' bedroom furniture. He still refused to leave. So, I told my attorney (who was by now officially hired with a retainer) to file the divorce papers and get us back into our house as quickly as possible.

We were now entering the third week as refugees at my sister's house. She was so kind to have the three of us and the dog there, but with her husband, four kids and her own dog, it was a little crowded. Even more concerning to me, however, was the constant fear that Paul was going to lose it and come after me - and maybe even all of us. I knew when I left that I was putting myself and my own children at risk, and that was hard enough to deal with. But the thought of also putting my sister's family in harm's way because of my own dysfunctional marriage haunted me even more. Years before, my father had given me a semi-automatic Beretta for my own protection. And I now silently chastised myself, firstly because I hadn't thought to take it with me when I left, and secondly, because of the possibility that something given for my own protection might now be used against me - and others. The irony was/is sad and rich. When my father gave me the gun, neither one of us would have *ever* imagined that it might one day be used *on* or *by* a husband who had become the greatest threat to my life.

All of this was weighing heavily upon me. And I was not oblivious to the fact that it was taking its toll on my sister and her family as well. My own fear and growing paranoia about Paul, and what he might do, made *me* nervous, which then translated into behaviors that were making *them* nervous. For example, every time someone would leave the house I would quickly follow them to the door to make sure it was locked. I would peer out the windows sometimes and give a suspicious look to cars that might be passing by the house a little too slowly for my comfort. They noticed all of these things, and never complained, but I could see that it was leaving a mark on them too. As I came to find out later on, all of this was causing them to see - perhaps in a way they had not before - that what had been going on in my marriage was far worse than they had known. New questions were being raised in their minds.

When you're stuck in traffic on the interstate, and you see four emergency vehicles come screaming past your car, you don't have to see the wreck to know that whatever it was, it must have been pretty bad. Just the nature of the response tells you something is wrong.

Something like that was going on within the minds of my sister and her husband. They weren't in my home to see and hear all that had gone on, but they were seeing the *response*. And that told them a lot, all by itself.

After a month at my sister's we finally got an order from the Court requiring Paul to vacate our home, allowing the kids and I to return. This news was such a relief. At the same time, it was also terribly heart-breaking. I certainly took no pleasure in knowing that Paul was having to leave what had been his home too. I knew it was a terrible day for him and not something he ever imagined himself doing. Nevertheless, despite the fact that I felt the loss for Paul, it did not mean I was considering changing my mind. The overall well-being of my kids had to take precedence over anything else.

In addition to settling the home situation, the Judge had also given us a temporary support order that granted Paul limited visitation rights. I had told the Judge that I did not need support for myself, but I would like for Paul to share in the responsibility of providing for our children. Unfortunately, but not surprisingly, Paul was not interested in doing so. And it wasn't that he didn't have the money. I had evenly divided our assets. There was plenty of money for him to work with. He just didn't want to. And it made me sad to think that the day would come when they would know that about their father, and it would be deeply hurtful to them.

Next Steps

Paul and I had been working together for several years at this point, and our office was located in a renovated apartment above his father's garage. Clearly, things were going to have to change - both with regards to our working relationship and the location of *my* office. It seems crazy to me when I think about it now, but Paul didn't see it that way - at least not at first. He thought the separation was only about our personal life and that we could just continue working together in the same office.

I had to explain to him that the separation was to encompass all areas of our lives. I told him he could keep doing the work that he was doing for my clients in the bookkeeping and payroll tax areas and could bill separately for his work; I would simply let the clients know what was happening so they understood. I felt pretty sure that my clients would be okay with this as long as the quality of work did not diminish. And, they *were* fine with it. As for the work, if anything, the quality *improved* because, for the first time, *the person who had been doing the majority of it had some sort of hope*. Having sorted that out, I then began pondering where I might go and, just as I was trying to figure all of that out, I was contacted by a dear friend of mine who knew my situation and, because she too had endured an abusive relationship, wanted to help me out any way she could.

Her help came in the form of some office space made available for me - free of charge. It was a timely and humbling gift that I will never forget. Encouraged and energized by her generosity I dove into the task of renovating her office and, in a very short span of time, had it ready to go. Getting back to work was exactly what I needed; it was a way of restoring some normalcy to an otherwise chaotic situation.

Meanwhile, back at the house, things were also changing - for the better. There was a different sort of "feeling" in our home with Paul out of the picture. It was just far more *peaceful*. We had experienced that "peace" before, whenever he was out of town for a trip, but it was short-lived, and we always knew that he was coming back, which cast a long shadow over those fleeting occasions.

But now it felt different. There wasn't going to be any coming back - not if I had anything to say about it. The peace felt more real, more solid, more *promising*. To be sure, peace wasn't the only emotion in our home - there was a lot of hurt and grief and confusion to come. I knew that. But there was a hope now that was just as substantial, and it was gaining ground every day.

Once the kids and I were back in the house, I tried to get back into some kind of routine as quickly as I could. Even amidst the rising hopes, I was still very upset about the situation....but I tried to hide that from the kids. I would sit on the back porch once they were asleep, and I would drink wine and *cry*. This went on for many weeks. I wasn't upset about my decision to get a divorce. I knew, by now, that Paul would never change, no matter how much I wanted it. It was *another* loss I was grieving. I was 43 years old and, as far as I could see at the time, I had given all of my good years to a man who never really loved me, at least not the way I knew that I deserved to be loved. Those years were gone, and I couldn't get them back. I would never have the "fairy tale" marriage that I had imagined as a young girl.

Alongside that, I felt horrible about the fact that I had chosen so poorly that, as a result, my children would not have a father who was present in their lives on a regular basis nor the family environment that I had always hoped for them. Those were the losses I was now mourning. They were deep and discouraging, and I dealt with them the best that I knew how. I was brave during the day and *broken* at night. And all I could do was just keep looking ahead to what came next.

It was around that time that a dear friend called me during the first week of August to tell me that Paul had called and asked him for the name of a good restaurant in Pass Christian. He was making plans to surprise me by renting a limo and going to some big, fancy dinner for our 21st anniversary. I already knew that Paul *wanted* to take me to dinner because he had previously asked - and I had turned him down. But I *didn't* know he had intended all along to go forward with his plan. Clearly, it didn't matter to him that I didn't want to. It didn't matter because it wasn't about me, it was about him and, ultimately *for* him. So, armed with the heads up, I continued to turn him down. In the end, however, he finally wore me down because it occurred to me that, if I *didn't* go, he would use it against me. He would, no doubt, paint a picture of himself to the children as the one who was trying to make it work, and me as the one who wouldn't even try.

When I finally gave in and said "yes", I let him know right away that I already knew about the limo and had no intention of riding in it with him but would drive myself to the restaurant and meet him there. When the night finally came, he completely manipulated me by making sure the limo showed up at the house at about the time I would have been getting in the car to leave. I was furious. He knew that he could back me into a corner and make me seem like the "bad guy" in the eyes of the children because I would not receive this gesture of *apparent* kindness and generosity - even though it was nothing of the sort. It was nothing more than a thinly veiled strategy to make himself come out as some sort of "knight in shining armor" and to do it in a way that would be difficult for me to turn down.

The next thirty minutes were just dreadful. Paul had purposely picked a restaurant a few cities over so that he would have time to interrogate me along the way. And he did. Relentlessly, he tried his best to make me feel sorry for him and, feeling trapped and not wanting to set off his violent temper, I just endured it. For most of the evening I was in tears, for one reason or another. When we arrived, I ordered quickly to get things moving along, but had no appetite. Paul, on the other hand, had a *voracious* appetite and was all too happy to oblige by eating everything I had ordered in addition to his own. Eventually, after a seemingly endless meal, we left the restaurant.

During the ride back, Paul, seeing that I wasn't buying into the "feel sorry for me" plan, switched tactics. He, instead, spent the entire ride back telling me about how happy he was with his life now. He liked having his freedom and emphasized the fact that he had no obligations. The irony was rich because, during our entire marriage, he had done his level best to offload any obligations he might and should have had. And then, as if that was not enough, he threw in a serving of his rampant narcissism (it was either that or sheer desperation) when he announced that he was actually *glad* to see me crying. He said it made him feel good because, in his willful obtuseness, it was a sign that I really cared. Nothing could be further from the truth, but then again, his perceived reality was just that – *perceived*. My tears were not those of a person who was broken-hearted, but rather of *frustration* - frustration over the outcome of this entire manipulative evening and frustration in the knowledge that there was only going to be more where this came from. The road ahead was going to get worse before it got better.

Despite these sad realizations, as the months progressed, at least one thing was getting better: I began to cry less. Partly because I was just worn out and didn't have a lot left in my emotional fuel tank. Also, some of it was because the hope of a different future kept breaking through the darkness, and it was having an effect on me. And not just me, but on my children as well. Just as they had done before, when Paul was away on active duty, they once again began to come into the living room at night and watch TV with me. We shared more and more meals together, and there was a new sound that was making its presence felt in our home: LAUGHTER. Imagine that...

Perhaps the clearest illustration of the developing change in our home was the occasion when, on one particular Saturday morning, I was in the kitchen washing dishes and, as my son walked into the room behind me, he stopped and called out to me, "Mom, you're *singing* again!"

His words went through me like a bolt of lightning. I instantly felt the significance of his simple observation and burst into tears. In that moment I realized that I HAD stopped singing - for God knows how long - and had not even realized it. In my earlier years I had always loved to sing while I cleaned the house or cooked our meals. And so, as much as anything else that happened in this crazy journey, this simple moment, that simple observation by my son, clearly brought into focus one of the many *effects* of my oppressive husband's behavior on me: *He had taken away my singing - and my song - and I hadn't even noticed.*

In that instant, I had more clarity than ever before as to what the cost of all this had been for me. As it turned out, that was just the tip of the iceberg. There were many other observations that would surface, unexpectedly, over the months and years to follow that would confirm, over and over again, how much I had been negatively influenced by my husband's controlling and abusive ways - and how much all of this had cost me/us.

The weeks continued to roll by and Paul would occasionally arrange to see the children. There was no regular or discernible pattern to it, and it felt very much that the deciding factor was whatever happened to suit him in that moment. One thing was clear: they were not a priority or, at the very least, they were not *enough* of a priority to become a regular fixture in his schedule. That, to me, spoke volumes. Sadly, as time would reveal, I wasn't the only one that was picking up on it.

Our son, not surprisingly, was more receptive to his father than our daughter was. And I understood that. It was sad to me because

I felt like he was committed to his father in a way his father was *not* committed to him. And he was committed to a man who would never be the sort of role model that he *could* and *should* have been for his son. But, again, I understood it - as best I could - and I tried not to get in the middle of their relationship.

For our daughter, however, things were very different. She would spend time with her father, but clearly did *not* want to be *alone* with him. As a result, she would only see him if her brother was there as well. To speak plainly, she was *afraid* of her father. His years of criticism, uncontrolled anger and violent behavior had left a permanent scar that, I'm pretty sure, is still there to this day. And seeing that has always been difficult for me. I can tell you that, on more than one occasion, I dove into deep bouts of introspection, questioning myself as a mother because I feel like my daughter's fear had developed on *my* watch. I told myself I should have seen it earlier, that I should have done more to protect my children. I told myself that I should have been more proactive and made this decision sooner. That's the problem with hindsight. Not only is it crystal clear, it is *ruthless* and, frankly, will beat you to death if you let it.

What cemented my perceptions in this area was a particular conversation my daughter and I had one evening during that period of our lives. We were sitting alone on the back porch and, in one of those moments where you are finished with one conversation and searching for the next, she suddenly said to me, "Mom, remember how I was always worried about you going on your ski trip with your girlfriends?" I said that I remembered. She asked if I knew why. I had always thought it was because of the 9/11 terrorist attacks….and that she didn't want me to fly. I was wrong. She chose that moment to express verbally what I had been observing for months: that she didn't want to be alone with her father because she was afraid of him. She explained that she always stayed in her brother's room while I was away because she felt safer with him nearby. She was afraid of her father's temper. I still remember the sick feeling in my stomach as she made her confession. I recall feeling overwhelmed with the realization that I had stayed far too long in my dysfunctional marriage. I felt the weight of my decision to remain in new ways as I discovered - on the installment plan - how much my decisions had cost my children. To be perfectly clear, Paul never *physically* abused our children; however, the combination of his uncontrolled rage and verbal abuse had left scars and damage that were debilitating. I would never want to equate physical abuse with emotional abuse - as if there was some sort of one-to-one ratio between them. They have similarities, and they have differences. But the *damage quotient,* I believe, works out pretty similarly in the end.

Getting Help

One positive result from these newfound realizations about the negative effects of our marriage on our children was that I was motivated to seek out help for them. I began to see that they *needed* to be able to talk to someone - someone that *wasn't* their father or mother - about the things they had gone through, the way they felt and were now feeling. They needed to speak to someone who, because they were "neutral", would not make them feel as if they were betraying one parent because they were speaking honestly to another. I was beginning to realize they needed a "safe space" to help process what was going on inside of them.

Sadly, my son responded much in the way my husband did and, after *enduring* the first appointment that I *made* him attend, made it very apparent that he would *not* be going back. And, while I think he could have - and perhaps still could - benefit from that, I don't judge him at all for his decision. I just *wanted* him to have every option available to help process and heal. I was just trying to be a good Mother.

For my daughter, however, it was a good option – actually, for both of us. We found a psychologist who was just wonderful. She proved to be an enormous benefit for us both and helped untangle and process a number of issues resulting from the abuse we had both endured. To be sure, it was not an *easy* process. In the end, however, it was eye-opening, educational, and, perhaps best of all, liberating. I learned a lot about myself and what a healthy relationship should look like. And I learned how to begin to forgive myself for all that I had allowed to happen.

In addition to the "life lessons" I was learning in this school that *no one* signs up for, I was also learning through reading, in a more and more focused fashion, books about abuse. I wanted to know *other* peoples' stories, not just mine. I wanted to see my own experience when compared with others to try and understand where my story fit in "on the spectrum" of similar stories.

My psychologist had strongly suggested this, but until then, as crazy as it seems, I had never really understood the definition of abuse. I would never have thought that my marriage *was* an abusive one. But the more I read and heard the stories of others and the collective wisdom of many, many years of heartache and struggle, the more I understood that, for whatever reason, I had been reluctant to use the "A" word in a situation that clearly called for it. To be sure, from where I stand now it seems painfully obvious, but I can tell you that from my perspective at the time, it wasn't nearly as visible. I now know better.

During that period of my life, I learned that abuse, whether physical, psychological or verbal, was applied by one person knowing that the other person is afraid of them, under their control or at least otherwise *capable* of being coerced or manipulated. Abusers use that fear to get what they want. This was definitely true in my marriage. Paul wanted things his way and would become angry very quickly when that didn't happen. The children and I had learned that, unfortunately. His job was to get his way, or else become unreasonable and violent when he didn't. Our job was to adjust to him and do whatever had to be done to make his world *work.* We had spent years walking on eggshells, making sure to do things the "right" way, which meant even when he *wasn't* angry, we were still controlled by his presence.

To sharpen that point a little more, let me say that many angry men will vehemently deny that they *are* angry men. They will say that they "rarely ever" lose their temper and, in their mind, that means they aren't "angry men". And when they say that, they are talking about the *frequency* with which they get angry - or not. And the truth is, they may not lose their temper all of the time.

But the devastation of anger is not just about the *frequency* with which it occurs, it is the *intensity* of it *when* it occurs. I previously alluded to this in Chapter Four, but I can describe it better in this unusual analogy. Suppose you come home one day after being at a soccer game with your kids and, as you walk in the door, one of your children takes his soccer ball and throws it across the room. And at the spot where the ball hits the floor - "BOOM!!!" - a *land mine* blows up! Fortunately, no one is killed but the shrapnel is sent flying and all of you were injured to some extent. And then, within this strange analogy,

the rules are that you have to live in this house -
even after discovering that it has land mines
beneath the floor! Would that knowledge change
you? Of course! Would it affect the way you
lived in that house, or moved around it?
Absolutely! What if days went by and nothing
else happened? Would you just go back to living
as before - as if nothing had happened? Would
you tell yourself that it was just an anomaly and
would never happen again? *Unlikely.*

And then, after a couple of months,
another land mine went off in another part of the
house. Again, thankfully, no one was killed, but
there were further injuries. How would you
react? What would that do to you? Would the
fact that "the land mines only go off every once in
a while" make things better? *Of course not.* The
knowledge of the *presence* of land mines that you
could not see or predict, but which were
certainly there, would forever change you.

I know, it's a crazy analogy because, in the
real world, that wouldn't happen, and you
certainly *wouldn't* stay in a house like that!

But if the "house" was your marriage and
the "land mine" was your abusive husband - I
think you see where I'm going. That's just a
glimpse of what it's like to live with an angry,
unreasonable and out-of-control man. Unlike the
analogy, you know where *this* land mine is, but
you don't know *when* it's going to go off, or what
the resulting damage will be. And it doesn't have

to go off all the time for it to have a completely devastating effect on your home.

I began reading a lot during this time. And the reading helped me to think about what was going on and offered me a "balcony" of sorts from which I could look down upon my situation - my life and marriage - and see it in a new way and from a different perspective. Perhaps the *best* book I read during that period was one by Lundy Bancroft titled *Why Does He Do That?*. This was the most difficult book to read, but, by far, the most enlightening - and heart-breaking. I cried frequently as I read, simply because there was so much that I could identify with and I found myself saying, "Yes, that's IT! That's *exactly* what's going on", or "that's *precisely* what it feels like." It was as if Mr. Bancroft was actually sitting in my living room every day and night. The things he described: how Abusers behave, what they do and say, and *why*.....it was amazing! I cannot overstate how therapeutic this book was for me and I have frequently recommended it since.

I took another significant step during this time: I started writing my story. My attorney had suggested I do so for a couple of reasons. Firstly, and practically, we needed to "make a case" for leaving my husband and, since Paul would never agree to divorce on the grounds of irreconcilable differences, I would have to demonstrate that I was the subject of cruel and abusive behavior that was damaging to both me and my children.

The second reason was because he knew it would help me to process what I had been living with and help me to deal with the pain and grief I had experienced - and was still experiencing. One thing I discovered through all of this, to my great surprise, was that I had managed to suppress or "forget" a great deal of what had happened. The more I wrote, the more I remembered. And the more I consulted with my dear friend, Patti, the more *she* helped me to recall things I had completely forgotten - and they were terrible things. How could I have "lost" them like that? I'm no psychologist, but I believe that a lot of it was some kind of survival mechanism I had developed. I think that, subconsciously, I knew that if I was going to stay in this marriage, I was going to have to bury a lot of scarring images - otherwise it would be too much. I would have been overwhelmed by the enormity of it and would not have survived. But now that I no longer was working to save the marriage, my mind could "afford" to dig up some things that had been buried for a while. Was it hard? My goodness, yes. *But* it was healing...

What I didn't know at the time was that there were more stories yet to come. I had no idea what sort of fight I was getting into and, frankly, was not at all prepared for what Paul was going to do once he realized I really *wasn't* coming back, and the divorce was imminent.

This is where things that were already ugly got even *uglier....*

<u>Seven</u>

By limiting Paul's access to the house, I had taken back some control of our home environment, which was good for both the children and me. At the same time, any gains that were made along the way were almost always accompanied by losses of some sort. The housing situation was no exception. Paul was extremely unhappy about having limited access and, in response, he began using the children to gain access when I wasn't around. He would play on their emotions and loyalties, making them feel guilty until they agreed to let him in. Every time they gave in, he would look around the house and take something of mine - something that usually meant little or nothing to him personally - out of spite.

On one occasion, after my son had been manipulated into letting his father in, something important was taken. What it was doesn't matter. What mattered was that my son felt badly about it and his father didn't care about that. He thought nothing about putting the kids in the middle of things they ought not be, or of making them unwilling (and sometimes unwitting) accomplices in things that they would never have chosen to be a part of on their own.

I told my son not to worry about what was done and tried to assure him that it was not his fault. How much of that he truly believed, I don't know. I went on to explain to him that I didn't expect him to stop his father. At first, I was going to tell him to "never allow his father in the house again", but I realized this was probably going to continue to happen, and it would not be healthy for my son (or our relationship) for him to regularly be caught in the middle of things as he wrestled with competing loyalties. It was not my children's fault that their father was manipulative and didn't mind using them to get what he wanted.

All of which illustrates one of the many difficulties of going through a divorce - namely, there's really no playbook. No two situations are exactly the same. What might be brilliant advice in one circumstance will be ineffective in another. You just have to figure it out as you go along, and you're *not* always going to get it right. I know I didn't. And so, we just kept figuring it out.

As Labor Day was approaching, I decided to rent a house in Florida for my kids and my parents in order to take advantage of the long weekend. On the Friday we were leaving, Paul called and asked if he could come by the house that afternoon and get his tools from the garage. I told him that would be fine but asked him to do so *after* we had left. I asked him if he needed anything from *inside* the house, but he said he just needed his tools from the garage.

Given his track record of taking things that didn't belong to him while I was IN town, I had no confidence whatsoever that he would not do something even more spiteful when I was OUT of town. For all I knew, I could come back to a completely empty house. Honestly, my concerns were about more than our possessions or the fear of having valuable things disappear.

To be sure, some of the things I was worried about losing were valuable, not just in a monetary sense but in an emotional sense...like the picture that my mother painted, which he had callously and heartlessly destroyed, is one that comes to mind. He had already shown that he was more than capable of discarding and ruining things that had deep sentimental value without batting an eye.

But beyond the significance of all that, the thing that concerned me even more was knowing that this callous person, who had become increasingly irrational, violent, and unpredictable over the years, had *easy access* to our home. And, as long as he had that, I really could never feel safe inside my own home.

For that reason, as well as in anticipation of him possibly taking and destroying more things that were meaningful to me (and my kids), I made arrangements for a locksmith to come by the house after the kids were at school and change all of the locks.

I didn't tell the children about any of this because I knew Paul would lose his mind when he found out, and I wanted them to be able to say honestly that they did not know anything about the locks being changed. It wasn't about being deceptive, it was about being protective of them and establishing some long-overdue stability in our home.

As he said he would, Paul showed up that afternoon and - *of course* - he completely disregarded what I had said and came *before* we left. I don't know why I believed he would listen to me. Doing so would have been totally contrary to his controlling personality. My asking him *not* to come before we left was like waving a red flag in front of a bull. There was simply no way he was going to miss an opportunity to have an *encounter* with me or to get in a little more emotional bullying at every opportunity.

I know that may sound a little bitter, and it probably is. But there was a calculated hatefulness behind so much of what was done by him during that time, and there was no other way to explain the behavior other than it being a deliberate attempt to be hurtful and cruel. As a previous generation would say, "It was just plain cussedness".

And so there he was right on cue. And I was a nervous wreck: afraid he was going to find out about the locks while we were still at the house, and all hell would break loose.

I quickly got the kids and my parents in the car while Paul headed to the garage to gather his tools. I stopped and asked him if he needed anything from the house. Again, he said "No." Turning quickly, I ran upstairs, set the alarm and locked the door. My heart was racing as I hurried down the steps toward the car. Without a backward glance, I cranked up the engine and took off. I don't think I started to calm down until we were many miles away.

Although we were safely on the road to Florida by now, I was still nervous because I knew the angry phone calls would be starting soon. There was no doubt in my mind that Paul would attempt to enter the house. Knowing that, I asked my son to hand me his cell phone. I told him I was expecting a call from someone and that my phone had died.

As you have probably gathered, my phone was fine, and I hated lying to my son. But I *knew* that Paul would call our son when he couldn't reach me, and I didn't want my children in the middle of the fury that I felt sure would be unleashed.

I put both of our phones on vibrate and continued driving. Sure enough, my phone started vibrating incessantly not thirty minutes later. Then, as I expected, my son's phone started vibrating. **Paul knew**...and he was furious. After dozens of attempted calls, the angry text messages started coming in, and they continued for quite some time. When we got to the rental house a few hours later, I called Paul and asked him to stop badgering us and to leave his son out of it. *Of course, he didn't.* After I hung up he *immediately* called our son and dragged him into the middle of the fight. It was a mess and could have, should have, been avoided, no matter how angry Paul was with me for changing the locks.

We still managed to enjoy our weekend away and, upon returning I was amazed to discover that Paul hadn't kicked the door in. He remained extremely angry about the locks being changed, but he had resigned himself to the fact that there wasn't a lot he could do about that. He also began to see that his efforts at manipulation were not going to work anymore. So, he changed tactics. As he felt me pulling further away, he began to think of ways to see me or "run into me". Paul began to show up at functions where he knew I would most likely be present, which was extremely unnerving for me.

By now we were four months into the "separation", and Paul decided that he was going to attend the annual neighborhood Halloween party. We had both enjoyed it over the years and so he knew I was probably going as well. Coincidentally, I had decided, by that point, to stop wearing my wedding ring. I knew I was never going to allow myself to go back to a controlling, narcissistic relationship. His actions since the separation had only proven that I was right to leave him. I needed to send him a message that I was moving on – one that he would understand. Paul noticed that I was not wearing my ring, and he took no time to come over and interrogate me about it. I told him that I knew he was never going to change, and I was not going back to the life I had previously lived. He then asked if he could have the ring back. Looking back, I suppose I shouldn't have been surprised by his question. Still, I was. And, as crazy as it might seem, it stung. And I remember thinking, "Wow…. is it really just about the money?"

The next week Paul asked if he could come and get some things out of our attic. I told him that he could come and get whatever he wanted. I had previously told him that he could have whatever furniture he wanted other than the children's furniture. So, Paul came to the house that Saturday and went up into the attic. After he was up there for a while, he came downstairs with something in a doubled plastic bag. He dropped it on the counter in front of me before he left. He had an angry look on his face. I asked what was in the bag. He said, "Shotgun shells." I said, "What are you going to do with shotgun shells? You don't hunt." Paul then got right up to my face and said, menacingly, "No, but I *might!*"

I was frozen with fear. It was a clear and undeniable threat, and I have no doubt that, if a police officer or a judge had been present to witness the whole thing, Paul would have come under immediate scrutiny. Nevertheless, despite the fact that it was extremely unnerving, I was determined that I was not going to let him get to me or see my fear. Without hesitation, I got in his face and told him to "Get out!" in the most stern and threatening tone I could muster.

It felt good to say it, and even better to see him walk out. After the door closed I let out a huge sigh and felt a wave of emotion come over me. Things were unraveling quickly...

Paul called me the following week and asked to come to my new office and backup some of the clients' information that he would be working with preparing their payroll returns and monthly financial statements. I agreed because we had previously decided he would continue to do this work for our clients as he had done in the past. I had no desire to take away his ability to earn a living as long as he did not harm the relationships I had established with those clients over the years. Paul showed up at the scheduled time, and I asked him what files he needed. I intended to save the data for him myself. He said he needed to sit at my computer to conduct the backup. I decided to let him because I didn't want a fight. He sat down at my computer and I stood behind him to see what he was copying. Paul began copying individual client Excel and Quickbooks files. I was okay with that, because I knew that those clients had chosen to continue to work with him.

Then he started another task and, before I realized it, he had started to copy the *entire hard drive* on my computer. I told him to stop, but he refused. I tried to physically stop him. We pushed and shoved each other as I tried to get him away from my computer. Paul pushed me up against the wall and started screaming at me. I told him I was going to call the police if he didn't stop. He, again, refused. So, I did exactly what I said - called 911. Paul removed his thumb drive from my computer, ran for the door and got into his Hummer (not the most inconspicuous getaway car). The police arrived, and I quickly told them what had happened. Immediately they jumped in their squad car and sped off. They stopped Paul a couple of streets away and, as I found out later, very sternly explained to him that he would be arrested if he came near my office again.

It was now late November 2004. I had left Paul in July of that year. Even though I already had ample evidence to support my case for divorce, the events of the past five months had only served to confirm my well-established conclusions. I knew, without a doubt, that Paul would never change, and divorce was, and perhaps always had been, inevitable.

During this same period, Paul learned that I had been seeing a psychologist. I had asked him several times during our marriage to seek couple's counseling and anger management counseling, but he had steadfastly refused to even consider it. The discovery that I was seeing a psychologist on my own seemed to trigger a sudden, "last-ditch" willingness on his part to see a counselor. I did not believe, even for a second, that his newfound desire for help was *really* about him wanting to change. It was, undoubtedly, a pragmatic effort to get a handle on a situation that was already well outside of his control.

But he gave it a shot and, out of the blue, told me one day that he had been doing so. He further alleged that this counselor had said that the two of us should meet with him together, as that was the only way any real progress could be made.

I was hesitant to believe Paul was telling me the truth, so I asked for his counselor's name and phone number. To my surprise, I discovered there really *was* a counselor that he had been seeing. Furthermore, he confirmed that he *had* told Paul that he would like to meet with both of us, but he also told me his *reason* for wanting to meet with me was partially because he did not think Paul was telling him the truth about what was going on in the marriage. He had told Paul that, in order for the counseling to be effective, he was going to have to tell him the whole story, and there was no way that was going to happen without me being there. So, after talking at length on the phone, I reluctantly agreed to attend one session.

The meeting was set for the following week. It didn't take long for the counselor to understand what he was dealing with. Right out of the gate, he asked me why I had filed for divorce. I proceeded to describe for him Paul's history of having a very short temper and his abusive behavior. The counselor then informed me that he had been told, by Paul, that I had a boyfriend. This was not true. I had been faithful to my husband. Paul then started ranting about how everyone in town was telling him I was leaving because I had a boyfriend. So, I asked Paul who that "boyfriend" was and added, a little sarcastically, that if "everyone" knew about my "boyfriend" then I guess I should too.

More seriously, I then told the Counselor, again, there was no boyfriend, and that Paul just needed to come up with another explanation for why I would leave him. His fragile ego and narcissism could not accept the possibility that I was leaving him because of *him.* He simply was not willing to accept any *responsibility* for his own failures.

The counselor then asked if I was afraid of Paul. I told him that I was, but not as much as I had been before. He asked if Paul had ever hit me. I said "Yes", which Paul quickly and angrily denied. I couldn't believe he was really going to lie about such an important issue. I explained, in detail, the times that I had been hit. There weren't a lot, but the fact there were ANY was cause for concern. I vividly recalled each instance, as if they had occurred just recently. Paul, suffering from a sudden case of "convenient amnesia" said he didn't remember any of them. I didn't stay much longer after that. I told the Counselor that he was wasting his time if Paul was not going to be honest with him, and I left.

More convinced than ever, I walked out of that counselor's office with my mind firmly set on moving things toward a final resolution (i.e., divorce) as quickly as possible. Sadly, "quickly" didn't happen as soon as I would have hoped. Not even close. In fact, it would take 4 ½ years to finalize the divorce and the property settlement - the divorce was finalized in February of 2006, and the property settlement was completed three years later.

Part of the reason for the delayed process was simply the fact that things as complicated as a divorce don't just get resolved overnight. The property settlement, in particular, proved to be a tiresome and tedious ordeal, for several reasons.

First, Paul had unreasonable demands. If you can believe this, he wanted *me* to pay **him** alimony, even though he knew that I had not asked for alimony from him. Secondly, he did not want to pay child support. And finally, he wanted all of the jointly held assets to be valued at unreasonably high values.

But the most significant, and infuriating aspect, of it - for me - was the fact that Paul had flat-out *stolen* our son's college fund. For years we had saved money for the children's college expenses. We had opened two certificates of deposit, one for each child, and we had managed to put away a significant amount of money for each of them.

Before the marriage had fallen apart - years before - I attempted to convince Paul that we should put our children's college funds into a trust that could only be accessed by them. At the time, Paul argued strongly against it and would not agree to do so. So, even though it was not the best vehicle for getting the job done, we stuck to the CD's, as Paul wanted – as *usual*.

Initially, Paul wanted to put both CD's in his name and each of the children's names. Since only two names could be on each of the CD's he said he would be the other name. I disagreed. I told him that I would be on our daughter's CD and he could be on our son's CD. I chose my daughter because I knew that Paul thought less of females than he did of males and, frankly, had always favored his son over his daughter, as much as it still pains me to say so. I never thought he would take his son's college money.

But he did. I'm not even sure what happened to all of it or where he spent it. I just discovered one day that it was gone. I was furious. Now that I knew what he had done, I made a personal vow that I was not going to ever give up on getting that money back for my son. And I didn't. It took $40,000 in attorney's fees and 4 ½ years of effort, but I eventually prevailed.

The fighter spirit that had been awakened years before was newly revitalized and had come back stronger than ever.

And I was never going to let anyone step on me again.

<u>Eight</u>

It was January 2005, and I had been separated from my husband for a little more than six months now. Even though I still had *years* of issues to work through, I felt that I was getting stronger and, because of that, felt more prepared for the long fight that I knew was in front of me. To be sure, I wasn't looking forward to the legal battles, and yet I knew it was a "necessary evil" if I was ever to get out of this abusive marriage.

As I gradually allowed myself to believe, and hope, that I actually *could* one day be delivered from this relational prison, you might have thought that I would have also started thinking about what was *next* - i.e., the possibility of finding someone else, someone with whom I could build the life I had hoped to build with Paul. The truth, however, is that I wasn't thinking about that sort of thing *at all.* The thought of meeting someone else, dating, getting married again, or anything like that was honestly the farthest thing from my mind. I had no intentions of ever getting married again. Even though I knew any number of men through my personal and professional lives that would have been wonderful "prospects" in most people's eyes, for me it just wasn't on the radar. Not at all.

It was during this time that I decided to reach out to a dear friend, Benicia, who I had met in Dallas twenty-one years earlier and who, in fact, is the Godmother to my son. From the first moment I met her we had an instant connection and have remained close friends since that time. Even after Paul and I moved from Dallas, I made sure to stay in touch and we ended up vacationing together with her and her first husband several times over the years. She was an easy person to talk to and also knew Paul well. I didn't have to give her a lot of the backstory whenever I just needed to talk with someone.

We talked for hours. As I opened up to her, she began to share with *me* things that had gone on in her own life, particularly the abuse *she* had suffered in her previous marriage. It was surprising and amazing to me; here I was talking with a dear friend whose story I thought I knew - and yet there was this whole side to her life that was completely hidden from me. She was just as surprised to hear my story. Two people with the same huge secret and yet neither of us had shared this aspect of our marriages with the other one. I guess we were too proud to admit to each other - or to anyone for that matter - what we had gotten into. I think we both blamed ourselves, in some ways, for not seeing things that we felt we should have seen before we got married. I know better now. But I wrestled with a lot of self-blame for a good while. At any rate, after we had talked for a while, she insisted that I come to visit her in St. Petersburg, Florida. She said she knew how hard divorce was and that I needed to get away for a few days to clear my head. I told her I would think about it. And I did just that.

The more I thought about it, the more the idea of getting away for a few days sounded like it might be just what I needed. As the Aussies say, "A change is as good as a holiday".

So true.

After about a week, I decided that a trip to Florida to see Benicia for a weekend was *exactly* what I needed. My biggest concern was leaving the kids for a few days, but I was able to get things arranged with some of their good friends, whose parents were more than happy to look after them while I was out of town. With that handled, I called Benicia to set up the trip, and she was genuinely *excited*. And it was infectious. For the first time in a long time, I had something *fun* to look forward to!

As the date for my trip approached, I received a phone call from Benicia. There was something going on at her son's school the day I was flying in, and she wanted to know if it would be alright if she sent her brother, Brent, to pick me up instead. I didn't recall ever meeting her brother, but she reminded me that we *had met* once before - when I first moved to Dallas in 1983. I was 22 then and he was only 15. The truth is, I still didn't remember him, but I told her that would be fine. She said that he might call me to talk and make sure I was comfortable with him picking me up.

The next evening, I received a call from him. I was surprised to learn that he was calling me from Maui, where he was on a month-long vacation visiting a good friend. I was expecting a brief conversation, but we actually talked for a long time. What I remember most about that first call was how sweet he was, and how he seemed genuinely interested in hearing about what I was going through. I remember hanging up – and wishing we could talk more. All of a sudden, the trip I was already looking forward to took on a whole new dimension.

All of this was taking place just as Mardi Gras season was ramping-up, which was typically a welcome time of year as it provided a much-needed diversion in the midst of the usual stresses of tax season. With the additional trials associated with my disintegrating marriage, the diversion was more welcome than ever. In those years, I would attend as many as four or five Mardi Gras balls, trying to make the most of the season. They were always a lot of fun and gave me the opportunity to escape my life for a little while. At that time, I was a member of four Krewes. Most of them were female organizations where the members – all of them women - could invite a male guest to attend the ball. In those organizations the women would be placed each year into one of the dance groups by the Officers. Your group leader would schedule practices and teach her group their "dance". This goes on for months before the actual event. On the night of the ball we all wear costumes and perform for the invited men and the audience viewing from the gallery.

And so, given all that was going on in my life, I jumped into Mardi Gras this year with full gusto. That, in addition to my typically insane workload during tax season, as well as preparing and thinking about my upcoming trip to Florida, left me with little time to focus on the divorce and the upcoming court battle. It was a welcomed distraction.

It just so happened that one of the balls took place the night before my trip. To my dismay, Paul had shown up - uninvited – and chose to stand on the edge of the dance floor and make me feel uncomfortable as he stared at me in silence. What normally would have been a great evening was ruined by his presence - again – and so it was a huge relief when I received yet another call from Brent. I used the call as an excuse to go outside and was afforded a brief reprieve from Paul's ridiculous behavior.

Brent had called to tell me he would be at the Orlando airport to pick me up the next day. He asked if he needed to come inside and help with my luggage, and I thanked him, saying I only had one bag and it was a carry-on. He told me that he would be driving a white SUV and that he would wait at Arrivals. We talked a little longer then I thanked him again and hung up. I returned to the ballroom and, even though Paul was still there, it suddenly didn't seem to matter. I remember having the biggest smile *that would not leave my face* - and I was totally aware of it. It was completely unexpected and certainly not something I had been searching for, but out-of-the-blue I found myself feeling excited about the possibility of meeting someone new. And genuinely nice. He had certainly been easy to talk to! Benicia had told me previously that her brother was single, good-looking and fun. To top it off, I would be in a place where no one knew me, a place where I could maybe let my hair down and kick up my heels a little. It had been a long time since I had done so, and it was long overdue.

The next morning, I arrived at the airport only to find out that my flight to Orlando had been delayed. I had Brent's number from the night before, so I called him to tell him the news and said I would let him know once we boarded and were ready for takeoff. That was it. A 30-second conversation, at most. But, just like the night before, this feeling of anticipation washed over me. The sound of his voice *did* something to me. This was something I hadn't experienced before. Why was I so excited about meeting a guy I didn't even know?

The plane eventually landed in Orlando, and I disembarked, heading towards our rendezvous point. I remember feeling foolish because, until that moment, it had not even occurred to me that I had no idea what Brent looked like! His sister had said that he was very handsome, but that wasn't a lot of help because, let's face it: there are a lot of handsome men in the world. And then there's the fact that one person's "handsome" is another person's "average". So, again, I had no clue as to who he was or what he looked like....nothing.

Eventually I made it to the doors leading outside and, as I stepped out, I noticed a good-looking guy standing next to a white SUV. I remember thinking to myself, "I hope that's him", but there was no flicker of recognition on his face, so I hesitated. "Maybe he doesn't know what I look like either", I thought. Maybe Benicia hadn't described me or shown him any pictures. I wasn't sure what to do at first because I wasn't about to get into a stranger's car, no matter how good-looking he was. Then I remembered I had his phone number so, trying not to look too obvious, I called him. When he answered his phone, he looked right at me – we shared a glance - and we both laughed.

After a quick greeting, Brent grabbed my bag while I got in the passenger seat. For the next several hours, while Benicia was attending the school function with her son, he took me on a tour of St Petersburg, which was really nice. It wasn't a date. But it *felt* like one, if that makes any sense, and Brent was the perfect host. As we drove, my initial jittery feelings disappeared and were replaced with a feeling of relaxation. During our unhurried tour of the city we talked about all kinds of things, taking turns finding out about one another. I couldn't remember the last time I had felt so at ease.

At one point he took me to a national park, where we sat and talked for a while. To my surprise, he produced a bottle of my favorite wine! (I later found out that Benicia had been telling him all kinds of things about me - including my favorite wine). After enjoying the wine (which was great) and the conversation (which was better), we left and headed back into town. Since Benicia still wasn't home yet, we went to a local pub to hang out a little longer. We had a few beers, and I enjoyed watching him play darts with a friend he ran into there. He was fun, and cute and a whole lot of things I hadn't seen in a long time, honestly. By the time we got to his sister's house for dinner, it was like we had known each other for much longer than a couple of hours.

We had a fabulous meal and, afterward, Brent took me downtown to a club to go dancing. I love to dance, and he did too, so - needless to say - we just had the best time together. When Benicia told me that I needed to get away, she was absolutely right, but I had no idea it was going to turn out like *this*. I was thinking maybe we would just go sit out by the ocean, which would have been fine. But what was planned as a retreat turned into a surprising connection. You couldn't have scripted a better weekend. It was just wonderful.

Indeed, it was *so* wonderful that it made me pause - a little. I couldn't believe how quickly I was falling for this guy *I had just met*. He seemed so amazing and, yet, I had been fooled before. His sister had told me that he dated a few women, here and there, but was not in a monogamous relationship. He was a bachelor with no children of his own. We had only just met, but I already felt more at ease *with* him and more valued *by* him than I had EVER felt with Paul. It seemed crazy to me. And yet nothing had ever seemed more *real*.

On Monday morning Brent had volunteered to take me back to the airport. On the way we stopped and had breakfast. Halfway through the meal, Brent picked up his phone, held it in front of him, and started typing and looking up at me. I asked him what he was doing. He said, "Deleting names." I asked if he meant "women". He nodded. I then asked him *why*. He replied, "Look, Christy, I have been dating for many years. I know what I am looking for, and you are the one. You go home, do what you have to do, and I will be right here waiting."

And just like that.... everything changed.

I was stunned. Did I just hear that? Did that *just* happen? Did he really mean that? My head and heart were racing. He seemed so wonderful, and we just *got* each other in so many ways. I couldn't believe he was really saying these things *to me*. (You have to remember, my self-esteem had taken quite a beating over the course of my marriage). And then I thought, even if he *does* mean what he's saying, do I really want to get into another relationship, much less a serious relationship this soon? Should I trust

another man and let him into my life? All of
these questions, and more, were running
through my head.

      I didn't know what to say. The only thing
I could come up with in the moment was, "Can I
have a little bit of time to process that?" And he
very graciously said, "Take all the time you need.
I'm not going anywhere."

      Wow. I totally did not see that coming.
Part of me was frozen. Another part of me was
screaming at the frozen part saying, "Don't just
sit there, say something. Don't let this get away
from you!" And so the inner turmoil continued
as we said our goodbyes not long after that. My
head was still spinning when I boarded the
plane. I wondered if I would ever have another
weekend that wonderful in my life. "Am I going
to find another man whose heart is any kinder or
sweeter than what I've experienced here in the
span of just a few days?", I wondered. I thought
about all these things, and much more, the rest of
the day.

      I was happy to be home and to see my
kids, and they were glad to see me too. I'm sure I
was grinning from ear to ear and, even though
they never said anything, I'm pretty certain they
had to have known that *something* was different
about their Mom. As much as I was relieved and
happy to be back with them, I couldn't stop
thinking about what had happened over the
weekend, especially at breakfast. I had told

Brent that I needed some time to think. He said I could take all the time I needed.

The more I thought about him/it/us, the more questions I had - not doubts, mind you - just questions: things I wanted to ask him. I wanted to investigate this possibility that had completely blindsided me. And I would have to be the one to initiate because, as I told him before I left, my kids could not find out about him - not yet, at least. If they did, and then slipped-up and mentioned him to Paul, the divorce would never happen or would at least become ten times more difficult. Paul would make sure of it. He was a very possessive man. If he couldn't have me, then he didn't want anyone else to either.

As soon as the kids were in bed, because I couldn't stand waiting any longer, I called Brent. I told him that I had a wonderful weekend and that he seemed too good to be true. He said he felt the same way. I asked if he was serious when he said he "would be right there waiting". As it turns out, he was *very* serious. I told him that I had a few questions. He said, "Okay, what are they?"

Here is how *that* conversation went:

> Me: "First of all, I want to know what you think about the age difference between us. You do know that I'm almost seven years older than you, right?"

B: "We are not in high school." (Good Answer)

Me: "Okay, well what about this divorce? Paul doesn't want a divorce, so this may take a long time."

B: "It's just a timing issue. We will get past that." (Okay, another good answer.)

Me: "Alright, well, what about the fact that I have two kids, 16 and 11? You have no kids and never have."

B: "If I am going to love you, I have to love your children." (Three for three...)

Me: "Last question, if you are as great as you seem, how come some woman hasn't snatched you up by now?" There was a slight pause and then...

B: "It's not like they haven't asked...." (Okay, that's hilarious.) "I was just waiting for the right one. *You're* the one."

Game. Set. ***Match.***

I remember thinking, "This is a total leap of faith. But how could I *not* take it? In the span of just a few days I had seen more of his heart than I had seen in Paul's over more than two decades. And I liked what I was seeing. We had the kinds of conversations I had been starving

150

for my whole marriage. Of course, I was very attracted to him and loved his sense of humor, but even more I appreciated the way he made *me* feel - like I was someone valuable, that I was *worth* listening to and getting to know. I felt like a person, not a possession. I'm sure at the time anybody would have said it seemed a little crazy. "It's too fast." "You're on the rebound". And maybe sometimes that stuff is true. But *something* just told me that I had to go for this opportunity and see it for what it was. A gift. A blessing. An opportunity to be loved - and to love right back - in the way it's supposed to be. I had started out believing I was going to live a fairy tale, then that dream died a slow, painful death, only to be resurrected and rediscovered in someone new.

And I didn't even know I was still looking for it.

We have been married since 2006 and that feeling has never faded. Sure, we're normal people - which means we can fuss and fight sometimes with the best of them. But even when we struggle, it's within an overall context of mutual love, respect and understanding, and a desire to serve and build up the other person - not tear them down. And so, even hard words can be spoken, without being harsh. Even difficult things can be said, but without being abusive.

When all of that happens in the right context - when there is a willingness to admit your faults and not keep score - that changes everything. That's the kind of fertile soil where love can grow BIG and roots can go DEEP. I love my husband, and he is even more precious to me now than he was back then.

With him I have learned what it feels like to be *encouraged,* and how very powerful that can be. It's more than powerful. It's transformational. I now know, experientially, what it is like to be in a marriage that isn't sucking the life out of you but is instead breathing life *into you.* I have had the rare privilege of being with someone who *wants* me to succeed, stands by me when it is hard, and rejoices in my victories - sometimes even more than I do! He is my greatest Cheerleader, my closest Companion, a wonderful Lover, and my dearest Friend. I know how blessed I am, and I thank God often for the happiness that was a long-time coming and is a part of my everyday life now.

A couple of years after we married, I was in my office and looking for something in a bottom drawer of my desk. I found in the back of the drawer a picture. It was a picture of Benicia (who was, by now, my sister-in-law), her three sisters and her brother, Brent. The picture had been taken at a family wedding, and Benicia had sent it to me many years before. I had forgotten about this picture. There he was...my good-looking husband. I couldn't believe it. He had been right there in my desk drawer for years. He had been with me all along.....

REFLECTIONS

If you've made it this far in the book, let me pause to just say, "Thank you" for taking the time and making the effort to do so. There are many other things I might have shared, which would have made this a much longer story, but my purpose in writing was not to produce an exhaustive memoir. My purpose was to share *enough* of my story that someone could read it and get a glimpse of what it is like to live in an abusive relationship - and *learn from it.*

I am under no illusions about the fact that there are *many* forms that abuse can take and that my story (sadly) is just *one* of them. Some people have experienced far greater abuse, some far less. The extent of the abuse isn't the point. It's that it still exists, and it shouldn't. And it is happening all the time, right under our noses, and usually off the radar until someone dies or is badly hurt or, as in my case, finds their way out. Even when you find your way out, you carry your scars with you. Abuse changes a person in fundamental ways, but it does not determine your future. Only *you* get to do that. You get to decide whether it is going to be a roadblock or a stepping-stone to something better.

I didn't choose to be in an abusive marriage, but that's what happened. I found my way out and, while I will not let my story define me, I will let it *drive* me. It's why I wrote this book - to tell my story in a way that encourages other people to tell theirs. Why? *Because abuse has to stop.* And the only way that is going to happen is if people *keep* telling their stories. By doing so, you will shine a brighter light on the abuses that are happening behind closed doors. So, if you're reading this book and you are one of the many who have lived through or *are still* living through the hell of abuse....

....find your *voice*

....tell *your* story

....and don't let <u>anyone</u> stop you.

That being said, I want to draw this part of my unfinished story to a close by taking a step back and reflecting a little bit more on some of my observations; things I have learned along the way. These do not appear in any particular order of importance and are offered in a more "stream of consciousness" fashion. My intention, by abstracting these, is to help some of the truths within my story become more portable and readily applicable, *especially* for those women who are still trying to find the door...

The "A" Word

Through my research on this subject, and through my conversations with other victims-becoming-victors, I am learning a lot about abuse. What I'm discovering is that abuse happens across all economic sectors, to both genders, to all ages, in all communities and countries. It does not discriminate...and is absolutely too prevalent. And it can take many forms. But despite the different forms, one of the most common questions that people seem to struggle with is "Why?" They want to know what the abuse is *about*. They want to know how a person can do this sort of thing to another person and still live with themselves.

That question has haunted me, too, and one of the most helpful tools I have come across is an insightful book by Lundy Bancroft titled, *Why Does He Do That?* It was through reading Mr. Bancroft's work that I finally gave myself permission to admit that *I was abused* and that my *husband was an Abuser*. Unbelievably, the word "abuse" never even crossed my mind when I considered how my ex-husband was treating me for all those years. Reading through some of the descriptions and definitions of abusive behaviors brought me to an emotional revelation that I *needed*. The first person I had to learn to be honest with about this whole thing was myself. At first, it was something that was embarrassing and humiliating to me (like I needed more of that in my life). But I have come to terms with it now and am no longer embarrassed, because I realize that **I** was not committing the abuse and, therefore, it is not **I** that should be embarrassed at all. More importantly, I needed to get comfortable talking about my past if I was ever going to be able to use my experiences - and what I learned from them - to help others.

So, if you're plagued by the "Why?" question - please do yourself a favor and read Mr. Bancroft's book. You'll be glad you did.

The Progression of Abuse

As I mentioned in the early chapters of my story, Abusers do not start off by hitting you on the first date. That's not generally how it works. And I'm not saying that Abusers have some master plan where they go searching for someone they can trap into an abusive relationship, although I'm sure there are exceptions to that. What more typically seems to occur is a systematic progression. Early incidents of abusive behavior are "successful" in that they get the Abuser what he wants. And because he was "rewarded" and got a payoff, with little or no consequences, he is encouraged to continue and feels free to push the envelope. His wants are met and, therefore, the outcomes encourage the continuation of the behavior that produced them. As the abuse continues, the Abuser learns what works and repeats those behaviors until or unless they start to lose their effectiveness, and then he (or she) may switch to a different or more severe course of action in order to get the same payoff. The law of diminishing returns is in full effect.

When I was going through my divorce and sharing some of the things that I had lived through with my family and friends, the question was often...."Why did you stay?" My answer was that I stayed the last ten years because I was afraid. He had told me he would kill me if I left him ... and I believed him. He didn't start out by saying those sorts of things to me, but that is where his threats eventually escalated. He had to work up to it. He also told me that I would never get the kids if I left. I could never leave because he would not let me take the kids, and I would NEVER leave them behind. Again, there was a progression and he got better and better at controlling and manipulating me, as much as I hate to admit it.

After asking me why I stayed in the relationship, the next question from those closest to me, typically, was "Well, what about the early years....weren't there signs? Didn't you see this coming?" The questions always came off as judgmental even though *I know that no one intended them that way.* I believe that they didn't spend a lot of time thinking about their own questions before asking. They were curious and didn't understand because they had not seen the abuses which were, for the most part, kept behind closed doors, especially in the early years. Putting that aside, I understand the questions. And, it isn't as if I wasn't asking the same questions myself.

But you don't know what you don't know. I understood that we had problems - serious problems. I knew that I was married to a man who could be verbally abusive, controlling and manipulative. And it was also true that he wasn't horrible every day. He could be quite charming when he wanted to be. There was just enough of *that* to keep me guessing and remain hopeful. That was also part of the manipulation. It just took me a while to see it because a big part of me wanted to believe better things and to hope for better outcomes. So, I just kept riding the "Merry Go Round", never knowing where I would be when it stopped and hoping that one day he would mellow-out and become the guy I had fallen for in college.

I wasted a lot of years which is one of the reasons I feel so compelled to tell my story to all women, but especially to *younger* women. I want them to be armed with the knowledge they need to be able to pick a good partner and to be equipped to more quickly recognize abusive behavior for what it is.

The Chain of Abuse

One of the things that has become apparent to me through my reading is that it is well-documented that there are patterns of abuse which are passed on and imitated in many family settings. This was certainly true in my own situation, but because it took a while to actually appear on my radar, I didn't see the patterns until much too late. I began to see that Paul didn't develop his own behaviors in a vacuum. And what really concerned me was when I began to see what he had learned being passed on to our son, as he would - in certain

158

situations - emulate his father - and *not* in good ways. As most young boys do, he looked up to his father and mimicked his behavior, whether right or wrong.

I first started noticing it when my son was only fifteen years old. He was beginning to be a little *too* rough with his sister. I also noticed that he would sometimes make broad, and very negative, generalizations about women. He would make a comment or observation, which he thought was funny, but were received as derogatory statements by me and his sister. I don't think he recognized just how his words were affecting us. To be sure, some of that was being young and needing more time to mature. But not all of it. Some of it was learned behavior that his father exhibited which he felt he had the right to copy.

Ultimately, I blame myself for that reality because I was the one who allowed him to live in a household with an abusive man for *way too long,* and it is one of the main reasons I finally left. I simply could not and would not allow my son to turn into his father and ruin his life, just as Paul was doing. Even though I *did* finally leave, I have lost countless hours of sleep chastising myself for not making the decision sooner. Thankfully, the subsequent years have given me assurance that my son is on a different and better path. Indeed, I could not be prouder of the fine young man he has become.

And, of course, I was equally concerned for my daughter - although for different reasons. There was never a chance that she was going to emulate her father. But his influence on her would take another form: namely *fear*. I did not realize just *how* afraid she was until I left him, and she told me one day that she never wanted to be alone with him ever again, because she was so afraid of his temper. And it was then that she told me just how much she had hated it when I would go out of town and leave her at the house with him.

I cannot tell you how awful I felt when she said that. I had been certain I was shielding my children from the negative effects of my first marriage. What I have discovered as I have emerged from naiveté is that your children typically know _so_ much more than you think they do. All the things you think you have hidden from them, a lot of which they figure out, is really the "elephant in the room". The collateral damage can be present for months - even years - before it is ever acknowledged, much less *dealt with.*

The bottom line is this: Don't stay in your marriage "for your children's sake". I know that might go against the grain for a lot of people, and I'm not saying there should be an unreflective, knee-jerk, across-the-board application of that maxim. But if you are in an *abusive* situation and the ONLY thing that is keeping you in it is the children, you need to think really hard about the damage that is being done by staying. Please understand, I know how hard that is and my respect for women in these situations, along with the courage and selflessness behind their choices, cannot be measured. And it doesn't help if your children are old enough to know what is going on and they start telling you how much they don't want "you and Dad" to divorce. Is it heart-breaking to hear that sort of thing? My goodness, YES! Nevertheless, and no matter how difficult it is to consider, you *owe it to your children to see beyond what they can.*

Sometimes, when you look really hard, you realize that the damage of staying has the potential of being so much greater than the damage of breaking-up the marriage. It is a terrible dilemma that, in a perfect world, no one should have to be in. But our world isn't perfect. And we aren't perfect people. Therefore, that means that sometimes the choice isn't between *good* and *bad* but between *bad* and *worse.*

At the end of the day you have to make the call. And neither I, nor anyone else, should *ever* stand in judgment of how someone decides in their situation. But if you are in an abusive situation, please at *least* give yourself permission to think about *not* staying and whether or not that, ultimately, might be the better choice. And don't just think about what that will mean *NOW*. Think about whether or not you might also be taking a step that will prevent the chain of abuse from continuing past your own generation.

Till Death Do Us Part

One of the many things I had to wrestle with, mentally, was understanding myself and trying to figure out why I stayed as long as I did in that relationship. I know many women struggle with that. But I wanted to know why. It took a while, but I finally figured out that one of the reasons I put up with what I did, for as long as I did, is because when I stood on that altar in 1983 and said, "till death do us part", I actually meant it. I made a promise that I intended to keep. When I said it, I wasn't just talking to Paul, or myself - I was talking to God.

And that, I believe, is a large part of what kept me in it for so long. I made a vow - to God, to Paul and to myself - and I meant it with all my heart. Even though I was in a terrible relationship, it *still* bothered me to think that I was somehow breaking this promise I had made. Unless you've been in this situation it's hard to explain that sort of commitment or sense of obligation. But it's real. At least it was for me.

So that was a genuine struggle for me until the day came when I realized that my decision to leave wasn't breaking up our marriage. The marriage was already broken because <u>he broke his vows first</u>. He had promised to love, honor and cherish me until death separated us. And he didn't keep that promise. On the contrary, he smashed it into countless little pieces, over and over again. It wasn't me he loved. It was himself, first and foremost. He loved what I did for him. He loved what I provided or made possible for him. But it wasn't *me* he loved. Nor did he honor and cherish me. Instead, he took countless opportunities to point out my stupidity or to humiliate me in ways that were deliberately calculated and cruel.

Once I realized that Paul had broken his vows it freed me to understand that my leaving didn't mean I wasn't taking my vow seriously. It meant I was taking his abandonment of **his** vows *very seriously*. If he wasn't going to care for me - and in fact do quite the opposite - then I was under no obligation to keep a vow that *was never intended to be kept under those circumstances*. You can't separate that part of the vow from the rest of it. When you break one, you break the whole thing.

He had promised to love, honor and cherish me. And if he wasn't going to do that, I would just do it myself.

A Good Fight

One of the things I have briefly mentioned in previous chapters is my childhood and how wonderful it was. It really was wonderful. Not perfect, of course, but I was blessed in that regard and I fully realize it. That being said, one of the things that would have made it better, quite honestly, is if I had been given the opportunity to see some "good" fights.

To be sure, I also never saw "bad" or unfair fighting - which was a good thing. But not getting to see two people struggle with each other in a healthy, grown-up fashion or letting us see them clean up the mess afterwards with contrition expressed and forgiveness requested and granted - in some ways, handicapped me. I didn't get to see that it was "normal" for couples to fight and, more importantly, there was a *way* to fight that was good and healthy and actually resulted in further understanding of one another. I never knew such a thing existed.

And so, because I had seen little or no fighting at all - I had no way to measure it. I had no point of reference that I could use as a standard to try and figure out whether what was going on in my marriage was typical or completely out of line. The simple *fact* that Paul and I fought, when my parents never seemed to, was troubling enough and often made me think we were "doing it wrong". But I didn't realize for quite some time just *how* wrong it was. If I had just once seen a "good" fight, maybe I would have realized it sooner than I did. I honestly can't say, and I certainly don't blame my parents. This is one lesson I hope you will learn much earlier and under different circumstances than I did.

Evil dies in the light, or at least gets severely wounded

I think the original quote is that "sin dies in the light". And what is true in the specific also holds true in general. The best way to fight abuse is to *talk about it*. A lot. It is getting much more attention these days in the media and that is a good thing. The "Me Too" movement is shedding light on the subject of abuse, AND it is hitting public figures where it hurts: their reputations and their bank accounts. And no matter where you are in this discussion, the increased public attention is making a difference. Those who engage in abusive behavior of any kind can no longer count on their victims staying silent and are being forced to think twice before doing it in the future. Their exposure is effective because Abusers, like most people, want to be seen as "good" people, not deviants, and that's part of the reason the media attention works. It sheds light on a truth that they don't want anyone to know. It's a closet they don't want anyone going into.

Obviously, they should have *better* motivations for stopping what they do than the fear of being exposed. But when it comes to abuse, I'll take a terrible motivation over *no* motivation any day of the week. It won't stop it entirely, but if public humiliation has an effect, I'm all for it until a better motivation shows up.

You Can't Change Someone Who Doesn't Want to Change

Do yourself a favor. Look in the mirror every morning and repeat this, "I cannot change *anyone* that doesn't *want* to change." We all think we can do this, or at least we want to

165

believe we can - and often with the greatest of intentions. But it's just not possible. Ask *anyone* who has dedicated his or her lifetime counseling people who struggle with various addictions, and they will all tell you the same thing - people have to *want* to change if anything is going to get better. Until someone gets to that place you personally *cannot* make it happen, no matter how badly you want it to. That was a hard pill to swallow, but after I had failed enough times I finally choked that one down.

Here's the thing: apparent "change" that comes about because of some external pressure, i.e., from some cause or force outside of oneself, isn't *change*. It's *manipulation*. It's a detour. It isn't real or lasting and will not deliver the results for which you were hoping. It's a mirage, and the closer one is to the source the more visible the "truth" of that failed reinvention becomes.

Why? Because if it's not a change of the Abuser's HEART AND MIND, it's just capitulation or worse, it's a *strategy*. It's a calculated maneuver where the Abuser temporarily stays the course because he or she can see that it will be useful to him or her to get what they want. And then, when it ceases to be useful, it will be discarded as quickly as it was adopted - cast aside like an old, worn-out t-shirt.

If and when REAL change takes place, it will most likely *not* be because of you and you'll never be able to take credit for it. We often times put so much pressure on ourselves to be the positive influence on those closest to us, but at the end of the day, who cares what brings about change? What matters – all that matters - is that something really *did* change from within the Abuser, and that's a good thing for everyone involved, including the Abuser.

When it's *real* you will know it. No one will have to tell you because real change cannot be hidden, or faked, and will not go unnoticed. That kind of change doesn't happen as often as we might all hope and pray, but when it *does* happen, it is a thing of rare beauty and a welcome blessing.

Years in an Abusive Relationship Can Change You

At one level, saying such a thing seems to be an exercise in stating the blatantly obvious. Of course, abuse changes a person. How could it not? But a distinction needs to be made here between the change itself and the actual recognition or *awareness* of the change. Usually the person who is changing is the last to know.

I remember when I was growing up, and our out-of-town relatives would come for a visit during Thanksgiving. It was invariably the case that, within seconds of pulling into the driveway and hopping out of the car, someone would exclaim, "My goodness, you've grown!!" And often it wasn't until that very moment that I even realized I HAD grown. A lot! It took someone else saying it to make me aware of just how much change had occurred.

That same dynamic goes on in an abusive relationship. Everyone is changing all the time, but the changes I'm referencing here are the particular ways that abuse changes you which, in its absence, might never have occurred.

So, as I stated in an earlier chapter, the day my son noticed me singing again - that was the first time it had dawned on me that I had ever stopped. Whatever has to be going on inside a person that causes them to *want* to sing, my abusive context had taken away, and I didn't even realize. Once it was made apparent to me I immediately wondered, "What *else* is different? Are there other ways I have changed that I don't know yet? What other things have I *lost*?"

Having said that, I should add that not all of the changes in me that took place had gone unnoticed. Some of them were deliberate choices brought on by my oppressive situation, which were my way of trying to manage the sad reality that had become my life. Specifically, there were some personal and professional aspirations that I decided to put on the back-burner because Paul had already made it abundantly clear how threatened he was by my success. I had conformed to keep the peace and, in the process, let go of my dreams for a time. But the "peace" I gained was only superficial. Inside there was turmoil because I knew I was letting go of pieces of me at every turn, and I hated it.

As I look back now I cringe when I think about what it all meant. And it leads me to say this: If you're in a relationship where you can't be you and/or aren't valued for *who you are* but rather for *what you do* or provide, or how you perform, then whatever that relationship is - it isn't love. If your spouse can't celebrate your success without feeling threatened or envious, let that be a warning to you. If the person you have to become in order to "make it work" bears little or no resemblance to the person you truly are - make no mistake - *the abuse has already begun.*

When I look back on that time, it saddens me to think about just how different I had become and what part of me was lost as a result. Not only was I different, I was deeply unhappy. The crazy thing is that I actually thought I had everyone fooled. In my mind, what people were seeing was a confident, happy and successful woman. And to an extent that was true. But not entirely. There were people close enough to me to know that *something* was going on, even if they couldn't put their finger on it. The confirmation of this was demonstrated by the fact that, after I finally got out of the marriage, almost daily people would tell me they could not believe how much happier I seemed.

This is why it is vitally important to build and maintain the kinds of friendships where people will say the difficult things to you because they love you too much NOT to say them. And if you want those sorts of relationships you have to constantly nurture them and create an environment where it is easy for them to tell you the truth. Because if you *can* build that support around you, then at least you will have another reliable set of eyes on your life that will hopefully see some of the things that are blind spots to you. I am very fortunate to have people in my life - true friends - that support me AND tell me things that I might not want to hear. That's how I know they love me. My group of girlfriends and I call ourselves The Vibe Tribe. I love them all for always being my true friends and for telling me things I *need* to hear.

The sad years are gone now and, even though I don't like what I went through, I don't regret what it taught me, or the person I finally became. As someone once told me, "Forget what hurt you, but never forget what it taught you." If you are reading this book and you are in an abusive relationship, I encourage you to *really* take a good hard look at yourself. Decide what it is *you* really want in your life. Are you the person *you want to be,* or is someone else forcing you to become what you will one day regret?

Don't be surprised if you can't remember everything

When I was going through the divorce, my attorney asked me to write down all of the horrible incidents that I could remember. So, I did, and, with the help of my dear friend Patti, I compiled a significant collection of them, some of which are in this book. As we talked about everything that happened, I found myself reliving those moments and feeling somewhat traumatized. It was a difficult, but necessary part of my healing process.

During this process it became apparent to me just how much I had *forgotten*. There were so many things that I had completely lost track of and that would have probably remained lost if it hadn't been for Patti's recollection.

I have no doubt that some of that is just part of what happens as we grow older. But I am equally convinced that some of it was my mind's way of protecting me - suppressing or just plain "losing" some of the terrible baggage that was just too much to carry around. I think it is not unlike what happens to someone who has suffered a traumatic accident - like my nephew who, after a terrible automobile wreck, lost whole caches of memory that have never returned. Emotional trauma can do similar things to a person so, if that's part of your story, don't be surprised that you can't put all the pieces together or remember every little thing. It's okay. You're going to be alright.

Abusers and Animals

Animals were not safe from the wrath of Paul. It didn't happen often but there were a number of occasions when the family dog was the unfortunate victim of his cruel behavior. There were a few times over the years when I saw his infantile rage coming on and was able to get between him and the dog before anything occurred. But I honestly have no idea how much it happened when I wasn't around.

In the end, however, I couldn't save our first pet, Sasha, from Paul's selfishness and stupidity. Sasha was a Samoyed. She had long, fluffy white hair, black eyes and beautiful white eyelashes. I loved her dearly. I did not know about crate training in those early years and, as a result, Sasha was never housebroken. That meant she had to live outside most of her life. Since we lived in the South, I would have her hair cut each summer, so she would be cooler, and, in spite of the heat, she enjoyed being outside and having the freedom to roam around the back yard freely. Before we moved from a house with a fence to one without, I asked Paul to promise that he would fence the back yard for Sasha. He agreed....but he never did. For months after we moved he kept giving me excuses and putting off the promise he had made.

I am crying as I write this...

Instead of putting up a fence, Paul set up a run chain that was severely limiting, confining Sasha to a small section of the yard. This went on for many months, and it was obvious to anyone paying attention that she did not like being on the chain and, I'm sure, must have felt like she was being punished. I truly hated seeing her on the chain, so I would let her off when Paul wasn't home.

It was during that time she began to lose her beautiful hair and, looking back, I have no doubt it was at least partially a consequence of her changed living circumstances and the resulting stress she felt because of it. A few weeks after her hair began falling out, Paul took Sasha to the vet while I was at work to see what was going on. He came home that afternoon, without her. All he said was, "I had the vet put her to sleep."

That was it. No explanation. No consultation. No chance to say goodbye - nothing. He just had her put to sleep. What kind of person does that? How thoughtless and selfish do you have to be? What he did was wrong - on so many levels - that it *still* infuriates me to think about it. Needless to say, I was devastated and have cried countless times recalling that day. I regret to this day that I was not strong enough back then to stand up for Sasha. I did, however, take care of our next two dogs and protected them from Paul's wrath. I don't know if "all dogs go to heaven" or not - but I truly hope they do so I can see Sasha again and tell her how very sorry I am.....

There's No Playbook for Divorce

Let me be clear, I am not writing this book to advocate for divorce, however, I do think it is necessary if you are living with an Abuser who refuses to change to strongly *consider this option*. At the very least, don't just automatically rule it out on principle like I did for so long. I don't say that to disrespect anyone's beliefs in this area. I know that some people have very strong personal/spiritual reasons for taking that position. And I respect that...I do. But I also believe that it is sometimes better to be in a situation where you have to ask for forgiveness than to remain trapped in a situation because you feel that you cannot first ask for permission.

And while we are on this subject, let me say this: No two divorces are alike. Yes, there are similarities in all of them, *and* there are always differences. But one of the common denominators is that there really are NO shortcuts to this process. The only way to get *out* of it is to go *through* it. Yes, it is exhausting and heart-breaking, but it is also true that you will have to go through it if you ever want to have a chance at finding happiness. And yet, as hard as the prospect of going through a divorce might seem, the cost of *doing* it will far outweigh the cost of *not doing* it – at least, that was the case for me.

Getting back to the point: there really IS no playbook for divorce. I, on many occasions, second-guessed myself. For example, regarding the matter of changing the locks on my house, I second-guessed myself several times. Should I have done that? Should I have told my children about it instead of keeping them in the dark to protect them?

There were many, many other doubts that plagued me over the years, and I am convinced that one of the biggest catalysts for all of that was the fact that, behind every single "*Should* I have...." question, there was this assumption that there WAS some sort of playbook and I was "doing it wrong". I wasn't. And if you're in the middle of a divorce - or heading into one - or merely contemplating it, remember this: there is no right or wrong move. There is only *your* move – your playbook - that hasn't been written yet. So just do what's in front of you. Take it one day at a time.

Financial Independence

I recommend in my "Girl, You Deserve Better" messages that women always maintain their financial independence by having their own career. Women who have no financial assets and career will have a much harder time leaving an Abuser. If you have your own assets, or access to jointly held assets, then you have the means to leave and provide for yourself and your children. If you have your own career, then you can continue to provide for the future. It is really just that basic. Do not give up your career or access to your financial assets. As a CPA, I suggest this to all my clients, male or female. As a past victim of abuse, I know how much easier it was to leave knowing that I could provide for myself and my children.

Do not misunderstand this message, however. If you are in an abusive situation and you don't have a career and/or the financial means to leave, don't let that be a reason to stay. There are resources available to you. Please see the **Resources** on the final page of this book.

Happiness is a Decision

Happiness is within yourself. *You can choose to be happy.* You can see your glass as half full and not half empty. I heard a story once that explains this perfectly.....

An elderly woman lived alone for many years after her husband's death. Her daughter lived in the same town. Her daughter was very good to her and always made sure she had enough money and was healthy. The daughter loved her Mother very much. The time came, however, when the daughter knew that her Mother needed to go and live in a nursing home so that she could get the daily care she required. The daughter was very worried that her Mother would be upset on the day they moved her to the retirement home. Moving day came and the daughter went to pick up her Mother and take her to her new home. On the way the daughter started describing how wonderful her Mother's new home was going to be. She described the beautiful gardens, the newly decorated rooms and the daily fun activities. Her Mother finally stopped her daughter and said, "I already know I am going to love my new home." The daughter was surprised and said, "But you haven't even seen it yet." Her Mother smiled and said, "I *know* but I am going to love it because I have *decided* to love it."

Happiness is ultimately a decision you make. It took me a while to understand this, but eventually I got there. The roadblock was that I thought happiness was an *emotion.* But it isn't. At the end of the day happiness is a *perspective*; it is a determination of how you are going to see and approach things.

I heard a saying years ago that went like this: "Life is 10% what happens to you and 90% how you *respond* to what happens to you." Truer words have never been spoken. If you are in an abusive relationship, you are certainly a *victim* in the sense that you are on the receiving end of some other person's actions and failures to act appropriately. But we aren't victims forever. *There's a point where the victim becomes a volunteer* as you choose to continue allowing someone other than yourself to have power over you and your future.

Do not allow it. Choose better for yourself. You *can* and you *must*. No one else can make that decision for you. Is it a scary choice? Absolutely. Is it easy? By no means. But it is simple at its core. And it is the choice you have to make and keep making every day when your feet hit the floor.

Your past has definitely *shaped* you. Never forget what it has *taught* you. But always remember this: It HAS changed you. But it cannot *define* you.

Only you can do that.

So begin now....find your happiness.

RESOURCES

Below are a few resources for those of you who are seeking help....I truly hope you find it.

For my fellow Mississippians:

MS Coalition Against Domestic Violence – mcadv.org
MS Coalition Against Sexual Assault – mscasa.org
MS Attorney General's Office – ago.state.ms.us/divisions/domestic-violence

National and International Resources:

National Network to End Domestic Violence (NNEDV) – nnedv.org
National Coalition Against Domestic Violence (NCADV) – ncadv.org
Rape, Abuse and Incest National Network (RAINN) – rainn.org
National Domestic Violence Hotline - thehotline.org
National Organization of Victim Assistance (NOVA) – trynova.org
End Violence Against Women International (EVAWI) - evawintl.org
Futures Without Violence – futureswithoutviolence.org

Additional Resources can be found on my website, girlyoudeservebetter.org